CLASSIC CYCLE CLIMBS

Yorkshire & Peak District

James Allen

THE CROWOOD PRESS

First published in 2014 by
The Crowood Press Ltd
Ramsbury, Marlborough
Wiltshire SN8 2HR

www.crowood.com

British Library Cataloguing-in-Publication Data
A catalogue record for this book is available from the
British Library.

ISBN 978 1 84797 762 5

All photographs by James Allen, except where
indicated otherwise.

Frontispiece: The author riding up Pea Royd Lane.
(Photo: Mark Jarvis)

Typeset by Jean Cussons Typesetting, Diss, Norfolk
Printed and bound in India by Replika Press Pvt Ltd

CONTENTS

Overview Map	6	
About the Author	8	
Acknowledgements	8	
About the Book	9	
Introduction	11	

Peak District and South Yorkshire

1.	Butterton	12
2.	Curbar Gap	14
3.	Deliverance	16
4.	High Bradfield	20
5.	Holme Moss	22
6.	Jawbone Hill	26
7.	Jenkin Road	28
8.	Longstone Edge	30
9.	Mam Nick	32
10.	Monsal Head	34
11.	Pea Royd Lane	38
12.	Pym Chair	40
13.	Scotsman's	42
14.	Stainborough	46
15.	Winnats Pass	48

West Yorkshire

16.	Cragg Vale	52
17.	Halifax Lane	54
18.	Ilkley Moor	56
19.	Jackson Bridge	58
20.	Meal Hill	60
21.	Mytholm Steeps	62
22.	Norwood Road	64
23.	Robin Hood Climb	66
24.	Shibden Wall	68

25.	Thwaites Brow	70
26.	Trooper Lane	72

The Dales and Nidderdale

27.	Buttertubs Pass	74
28.	Fleet Moss	78
29.	Guise Cliff	80
30.	Hartwith Bank	82
31.	Langbar	84
32.	Langcliffe Scar	86
33.	Malham	88
34.	Oxnop Scar	90
35.	Park Rash	92
36.	Trapping Hill	94
37.	Turf Moor	96

North Yorkshire Moors and Wolds

38.	Acklam Brow	98
39.	Black Brow	100
40.	Blakey Bank	102
41.	Carlton Bank	104
42.	Egton Moor	106
43.	Glaisdale Head	108
44.	Heygate Bank	110
45.	Murton Bank	112
46.	Robin Hood's Bay	114
47.	Rosedale Chimney	116
48.	Sneck Yate Bank	118
49.	Street Hill	120
50.	White Horse Bank	122

	Bike Shops	*124*

Yorkshire & Peak District Cycle Climbs

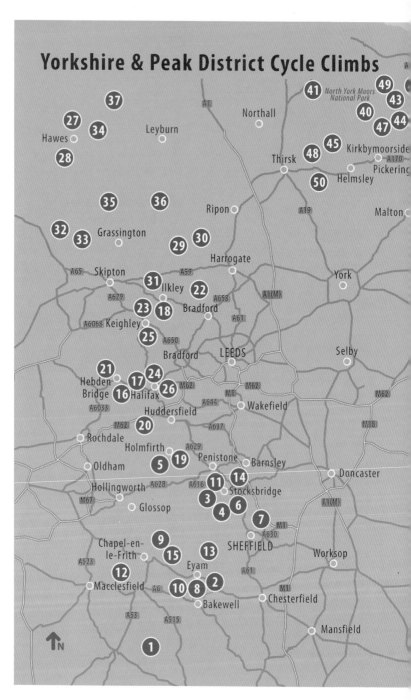

1 Butterton
2 Curbar Gap
3 Deliverance
4 High Bradfield
5 Holme Moss
6 Jaw Bone
7 Jenkin Road
8 Longstone Edge
9 Mam Nick
10 Monsal Head
11 Pea Royd Lane
12 Pym Chair
13 Scotsman's
14 Stainborough
15 Winnats Pass
16 Cragg Vale
17 Halifax Lane
18 Ilkley Moor
19 Jackson Bridge
20 Meal Hill
21 Mytholm Steeps
22 Norwood Road
23 Robin Hood Climb
24 Shibden Wall
25 Thwaites Brow

26 Trooper Lane
27 Buttertubs Pass
28 Fleet Moss
29 Guise Cliff
30 Hartwith Bank
31 Langbar
32 Langcliffe Scar
33 Malham
34 Oxnop Scar
35 Park Rash
36 Trapping Hill
37 Turf Moor
38 Acklam Brow
39 Black Brow
40 Blakey Bank
41 Carlton Bank
42 Egton Moor
43 Glaisdale Head
44 Heygate Bank
45 Murton Bank
46 Robin Hood's Bay
47 Rosedale Chimney
48 Sneck Yate Bank
49 Street Hill
50 White Horse Bank

ABOUT THE AUTHOR

James has been interested in the outdoors and fitness from an early age. He started mountain biking as a teenager, but turned to road cycling as an adult to strengthen the leg muscles following a cruciate knee injury. Since then he has taken part in a range of road cycling events including sportives, time trials and road races. However, he has a particular liking for hill climb events due to their purity, but also their severity. He enjoys training and rides around 10,000 miles per year.

In the past James has also been a triathlete and competed at Ironman UK Triathlon in 2008. He has also completed a number of large cycling events on the continent including La Marmotte. James holds a degree in Physical Education and a Post-Graduate Certificate in Sport and Exercise Science. Finally, and most importantly, he is a father and devoted husband.

Photo: Flaming Photography.

ACKNOWLEDGEMENTS

I could not ride my bike to the extent that I do, and I would never have been able to write this book, if it weren't for my beautiful, patient, resourceful and (currently) pregnant wife Jane. She has been a solid support through all my riding and racing.

I must also thank my three-year-old boy who has also shown great patience during the many hours I have been tapping away at the laptop rather than playing with him. I owe you Tom, especially for your cheers in the cold autumn rain during hill climb races. 'Nan-Nan Doreen' has also been a magnificent support over the years at races. Your encouragement has been invaluable.

In the cycling community there are far too many people to mention. However, I would like to say a collective thanks to all who know me through cycling, because you are a major reason that this sport is as enjoyable and rewarding as it is. Through injury, defeat, good times and triumph, the cycling community are a fantastic and incredibly supportive bunch. It's a pleasure to be a cyclist. Specific thanks must go to a few friends who have helped me research and produce this book. Simon Jackson, Danny Lowthorpe, Matt Newton, Neil Bentley, Mayur Ranchordas, and my brother Keven Allen have all been patient whilst I have waffled on about hill climbs. They have taken the time to be photographed or help with research when asked so I am much obliged.

Finally, and most fundamentally, I am grateful for the support of my wonderful parents who have supported me consistently throughout my life. To my mum who is the most gentle, measured and emotionally intelligent person I know: you are a template for my life. And to my dad, who is the essential structure and the inspiration for my writing and working life. I love your passion for written words and I have learned so much from you. Indeed, if it were not for you, I wouldn't have the skills or confidence even to attempt to write a book.

I dedicate this book to my Dad and to my wife.

ABOUT THE BOOK

The book is divided into four sections: The Peak District and South Yorkshire; West Yorkshire: The Dales and Nidderdale; and North Yorkshire Moors and Wolds. These four sections are colour-coded for ease of reference.

Each description starts with a table of facts about the climb, including a difficulty rating out of 10 within the context of the 50 climbs listed in the book. Also included is the address of a local café or tearoom where tired riders can compare their own experience over a tea or coffee and slice of cake.

Difficulty	●●●●●●●●◐○
Distance	1.5km
Av. Gradient	11%
Max. Gradient	20%
Height Gain	167m
Start Point	Hooleyhey Lane crossing with Todd Brook GR: 983763 (OS Landranger: 118)
Local Cafés	Yellow Teapot Café, Smith Lane, Rainow, Macclesfield SK10 5XJ ☎ 01625 574878

The map shows the start and finish point of the climb and the route it follows. We would recommend taking an OS map or a GPS system to help in plotting your route in more detail.

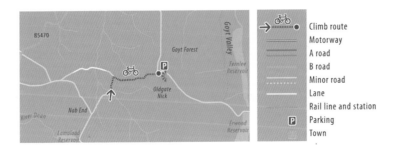

At the end of the book is a list of bike shops in the region, organised in book order. Each bike shop relates to one or more of the climbs so there'll be one nearby if you're in need of spares, repairs or just some good local advice.

INTRODUCTION

How do you select fifty of the best climbs in the Peak District and Yorkshire? The whole area is littered with hills and choosing only fifty is no mean feat. In the case of those described here, I have aimed for climbs that are amongst the toughest, but toughness is not the only criterion. The climbs also have to be iconic, remarkable or simply a joy to ride. Indeed, there are some climbs in this book that give an intrinsic thrill for reasons that are not always completely evident. I have therefore tried to mix instinct with rational decision-making when choosing the best. I have no doubt there will be many readers who may have different opinions about what makes a classic climb, but that's all part of the fun.

Each climb has been given a score out of ten in terms of its difficulty. This is also a debatable aspect of each climb because there are many variables that can influence how challenging an ascent is on a particular day. Wind direction, temperature, fatigue, mental approach, fear and a rider's equipment all play a part in how a climb is perceived. A bike's gearing is also crucial as smaller gears will allow most to climb some of the steepest slopes if taken slow enough. Indeed, even a 30% slope, although frightening, is not completely destructive if it is relatively short, then followed by an easier stretch. It's not that it's ever easy – it's just slightly more attainable. However, with conventional gearing some climbs become extremely difficult, especially if the slope is sustained around a 20% gradient for 200 metres or more. On such slopes most riders, regardless of fitness, will be close to (or beyond) their limit for enough time to make it seriously unpleasant. This is what I believe makes the toughest of climbs.

Another factor in selecting climbs for inclusion in this book is the overall experience when riding them. This is even more subjective than difficulty level, but it is a key aspect of what makes a 'classic'. It might be a climb's spectacular surroundings or the dynamics of the road that make it particularly enjoyable. It might also be that top riders from the past have left their mark, so there is the buzz of riding on the same tarmac. Or it could just be that 'x-factor' separating it from the countless others that might warrant inclusion.

It's enjoyable to analyse and discuss climbs, but the real pleasure comes from riding them. Indeed, I hope this book reveals my enthusiasm for cycling and the challenge of riding hills. Setting off with the goal of riding one of the hardest climbs then reaching the summit amongst some of the finest scenery in the world is truly gripping. Enjoy the ride!

I. BUTTERTON

Difficulty	●●●●●●●◐○○
Distance	0.7km
Av. Gradient	12.7%
Max. Gradient	23%
Height Gain	92m
Start Point	Wetton Mill; Easton end of Wetton Road in Manifold Valley. GR: 095561 (OS Landranger 119)
Local Cafés	Wetton Mill Tea Rooms, Wetton Mill Road, Manifold Valley, Nr Ashbourne, DE6 2AG ☎ 01298 84838

The Dovedale and Manifold valleys in the Southern Peak District are simply breathtaking. Few places are so scenic and tranquil, and there is a glut of superb climbs to have a crack at.

This climb, one of the most demanding in the area, leaves the gently flowing River Manifold and soars rapidly into Staffordshire towards the quaint village of Butterton. The approach to the climb takes you along the valley floor alongside the River Manifold. Rapid upward progress begins almost immediately as you turn off the valley lane following the signs to Butterton. You are propelled quickly to a double-digit incline

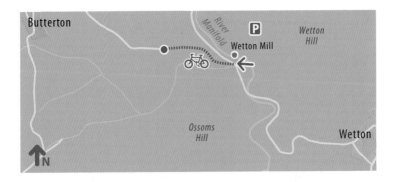

over the first 100 metres, in stark contrast to the approach. Yet a more substantial blow lurks around the next right-hand corner.

You are led into a dark, tunnel-like cutting where the road steepens considerably towards 23%. Meanwhile, the trees overhang and the close confines rise several metres above, enclosing upon you and creating a sense of claustrophobia. You really have to battle with the bike to overcome this short but brutal section because the remaining route is a joy. This begins as you exit the cutting and your attention is quickly drawn to the surprise view opening to your right. The Manifold Valley now lies far beneath and verifies the remarkable rate of climb you have achieved so far. Impressive triangular and dome-shaped hills are now at eye level, providing considerable satisfaction despite the fact that much of the climb remains.

The climb continues with a seriously steep incline for 100 metres as views now open to your left. Soon some respite allows you an opportunity to absorb some of this splendour. The climb passes through a typical rural scene with moss-covered dry stone walls and patchwork fields. Trees overhang the road and there is one more steep pitch into double figures before the final stretch. The road becomes bumpy (nothing too damaging); a small farm building appears on the left and a lay-by marks the end of the ascent. It's a chance for a breather before you roll through Butterton or return to the valley to sample another of the classic climbs close by.

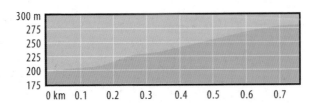

2. CURBAR GAP

Difficulty	●●●●●●●●○○
Distance	1.6km
Av. Gradient	11.3%
Max. Gradient	18%
Height Gain	181m
Start Point	South-western end of Curbar Lane at junction with Dukes Drive by All Saints Church, just off A623 Baslow Road. GR: 247745 (OS Landranger: 119)
Local Cafés	Palmers Café, Baslow Road, Calver S32 3XH ☎ 01433 631111

The old Roman road and former packhorse route, which climbs through Curbar village towards the skyline, is both picturesque and testing in equal measure. From the turn into Curbar Lane there is no hesitation as you are taken directly upwards on a strenuous opening. The gradient hovers consistently around 18% as you pass benches strategically placed to provide a breather for anyone walking to the village above. It's important to hold a little in reserve here, as you can easily go too hard on this first 200 metres and pay for it later. The road then bends right after this very steep start, entering the small village of Curbar where you can catch your breath a little and prepare for the second part of the climb. The slope remains challenging at 6–10% but it is enough to allow the legs to turn more freely as the wild moorland appears beyond the houses up ahead.

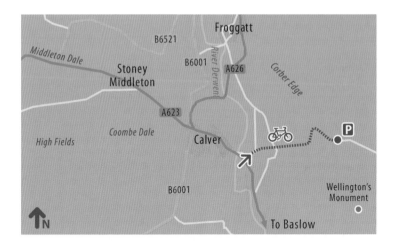

The distinctive 'V' formed by the gap between Curbar and Baslow Edges now draws you towards the summit, but there is still some way to go as the road winds its way up the hillside past huge gritstone boulders. The next 200 metres becomes very steep again at around 13% whilst the spectacular crags towering impressively above. This gives you some indication of the vertical height yet to be climbed, so with only 400 metres of road remaining before the summit, the steep 16% gradient on the next right-hand bend is inescapable.

The final slope is more exposed, but now offers fabulous views to the south towards the Chatsworth Estate. The route is now straight and comparatively sustained at roughly 10%. This is where you will encounter a carnival atmosphere if you should find yourself at the BUCS hill climb, where students in fancy dress demand a final, last-gasp effort from the riders. Even without these crazed academics to encourage you, with the finish so close you may summon the reserves to make a final strong push towards the crest of the hill. There is a subtle increase in steepness to 15% as you approach, but this is short-lived and as you find yourself within Curbar Gap itself the climb is complete.

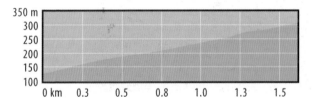

3. DELIVERANCE

Difficulty	⬤⬤⬤⬤⬤⬤⬤⬤◖○
Distance	1km
Av. Gradient	13.1%
Max. Gradient	23%
Height Gain	130m
Start Point	Mortimer Road crossing with Ewden Beck GR: 242968 (OS Landranger: 110)
Local Cafés	Bank View Café, Langsett, Stocksbridge, Sheffield S36 4GY (on A616) ☎ 01226 762337

Some cycling climbs hold a special place in the psyche of local riders and might even be given a name that reflects its character. Such a climb can be found at Ewden Bank on the Strines Road in the Dark Peak. Forming the final and toughest of a series of challenging ascents over the Strines Moor, Ewden Bank is affectionately known to many as 'Deliverance'.

The Strines Road itself is a staple in the training diet of regional cyclists. The grippy road surface and abrupt climbs sap energy with only the briefest respite found on the descents. The toughest direction to follow the 10-mile route runs south to north. It is bookended by the A57 and A616, with the Queen climb becoming visible clinging to the hillside after 6 miles. The name 'Deliverance' was in fact coined in relation to the 1972 movie of the same name reflecting the anxiety, panic and terror of the story, although the name is of course open to interpretation.

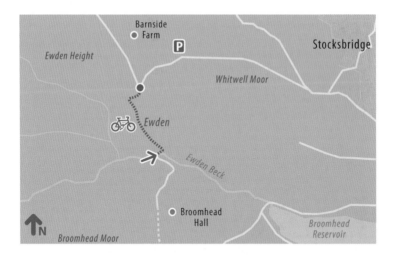

Following a sharp descent towards the darkness of Ewden Beck a right-hand; often greasy, hairpin bend quickly slows your momentum and you must immediately begin to pedal hard to establish a tempo. Stay seated if possible through the daunting confines of Broomhead Wood. Try not to be too alarmed if you have already sought the sanctuary of the easiest gear, but avoid going too hard because the most extreme section of 'Deliverance' comes next.

A steep left-hand bend forces you to rise from the saddle and take a wide approach, so be alert for descending traffic. The rough road steepens to 23% and progress becomes severely laboured, which can lead to concerns about inadequate fitness or poor form. It's important to remain optimistic for this next 150 metres, because after the emergence from Broomhead Wood the incline becomes more manageable. The climb now passes Yewtrees Cottage and the gradient here is as forgiving as 'Deliverance' will allow, so try to recover a little before the final summit.

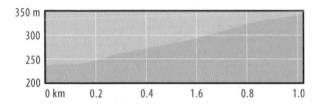

Beyond Yewtrees Cottage, most riders will have been duelling with the slope for several minutes but this is where Deliverance makes a final attempt to hurt you. The road subtly inclines towards 15% forcing another rise from the saddle. This next 250 metres is increasingly exposed to demoralising westerly winds, yet the final 90-degree, right-hand bend is now visible. The gradient is still steep for the final stretch, but the prevailing wind can now offer welcome assistance for the final dance on the pedals to the summit. Take a moment here to savour the dramatic landscape to the south.

THE TOUR OF BRITAIN ON STRINES MOOR

The Strines Road, actually named Mortimer Road, was once a turnpike or toll road and it was here that some of the world's top cyclists paid a heavy price in terms of their overall ambitions in the 2006 Tour of Britain. The savage inclines caused a key split in the peloton on a wet September day on Stage 3 from Bradford to Sheffield. The course that day took the riders on a 180-kilometre route with barely an inch of flat terrain. By the time the riders reached Langsett, the favourites had assembled at the front ready to do battle on the challenging slopes to come. The final selection at the start of the Strines Road comprised around forty riders including World Champion Tom Boonen, Nick Nuyens, Filippo Pozzato, Michael Rogers and a youthful Andy Schleck. Strines Moor was the scene of military live firing exercises during the Second World War and it was approaching Ewden Bank that the race fireworks began again.

Unfortunately, on the descent of Ewden Bank as the already steep slope dips quickly and exceeds 20%, World Champion Tom Boonen crashed. He misjudged the changing gradient and sharp corner putting him out of contention. Spectators expecting him to be at the front on the steep exit to Ewden Beck instead saw him receiving treatment from his team car. This serves as a warning to non-professionals to treat the roads and descents with respect, especially when it's wet. Following Tom Boonen from Ewden Beck was a young Mark Cavendish who, as a sprinter, was like a fish out of water on this terrain. However, he persevered dressed in his pink T-Mobile kit, which appeared bright amongst the gloom of the woodland on this miserable rainy day.

After Ewden Beck only fourteen riders were left in the front group including British riders Russell Downing and Kristian House. Not far behind in twentieth place was Ian Stannard in his Great Britain Academy kit. He was riding precociously considering his age and huge frame unsuited to such steep climbs. The front group was now established and as the race headed towards Sheffield, Filippo Pozzato attacked on the final climb of the day. He rode away to win and proved himself the best rider on the day, yet crucially it was the Strines Road that had thinned the front group forcing the selection of the strongest riders in the race.

4. HIGH BRADFIELD

Difficulty	●●●●●●●●◑○
Distance	0.8km
Av. Gradient	11.6%
Max. Gradient	30%
Height Gain	90m
Start Point	Low Bradfield: Junction of Woodfall Lane and The Sands. GR: 264920 (OS Landranger: 110)
Local Cafés	Schoolrooms Café, Mill Lee Road, Low Bradfield S6 6LB ☎ 0114 285 1920

The tiny village of High Bradfield is situated on a picturesque hillside just inside the Peak District.

This short but rigorous test begins in Low Bradfield, passing the cricket green then turning right at the signpost indicating ½ mile to High Bradfield. The first 250 metres take you past open fields on a straight road where the church can be seen high above. The slope here is a steady 8% but then as you hit the trees ahead the road quickly rears up. This is where the climb gets super-hard and will be so until the top, so you will need to show some real doggedness for the next few minutes.

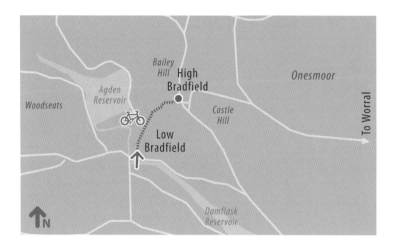

A left, then a right-hand bend take you to 30% where you will heave hard on the handlebars, giving every ounce of effort. The next 100 metres are relentless, sustaining an incline of 25% as the church appears again to your left. It's closer this time, but still agonisingly far away at this stage in proceedings. The road does begin to level out a little to 18% as the road bends left which seems like a small mercy considering what has been completed thus far, but the rough surface provides another challenge to negotiate.

You are now almost at the top and the road relents slightly for a very short time before the remaining push to the top. If you have anything left in the tank it is time to use it as the road returns to the default setting of 20%. This is mercifully short until you reach a T-junction where the gradient immediately eases and you can afford to sit down and relax your leg, arm and back muscles. You have several options for your next destination including a continuation of the climb towards Kirk Edge Road, which adds a further 800 metres at 10% towards Worral and Oughtibridge. Yet whichever direction you go, it isn't flat for long.

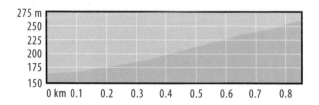

5. HOLME MOSS

Difficulty	●●●●●●●●◑○
Distance	4.5km
Av. Gradient	7.4%
Max. Gradient	14%
Height Gain	353m
Start Point	Holmbridge: Woodhead Road (A6024) at junction with Bank Lane. GR: 121067 (OS Landranger: 110)
Local Cafés	Penny Lane Café. 14c Daisy Lane, off Towngate, Holmfirth HD9 1HA ☎ 01484 688151

Holme Moss is Yorkshire's Alpe d'Huez and arguably the most iconic British climb of all. With its slope continuing much further than most other conventionally short and steep British climbs, it has been used in many classic races. In fact, Holme Moss is akin to the classic mountain climbs on the continent, albeit in miniature. The switchbacks on the climb also give it an alpine feel and what Holme Moss lacks in distance compared to its European cousins, it makes up for in terms of exposure to the elements. Holme Moss should be on your bucket list.

A warm-up for the climb is provided by the 2.5 kilometre approach from the market town of Holmfirth. As you ride casually along you will catch the odd, intimidating (yet exhilarating) glimpse of the ascent on the distant horizon. At Holmbridge the tough

stuff begins as you are thrown headfirst into part one of the climb and the road ramps to around 14% for a hard 200-metre period. This is slightly reminiscent of Alpe d'Huez where the long drag along the Romanche valley quickly transforms into a famously steep ascent up the mountainside.

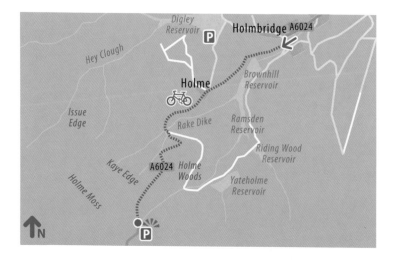

The slope relents to 10% for a short period then further to 4% for 200 metres, providing a little breathing space. Unsurprisingly, the ascent is not this easy for long, and the gradient increases then hovers around 10% for the next 600 metres taking you to the village of Holme. The ride through the village provides no serious obstacle and the moorland views become increasingly dramatic as you approach the second section of the climb.

A short dip then a left-hand bend takes you into the belly of the beast where the climb begins again at a continuous 11%. The surface of the road is now damaged and steals your momentum as you twist left then right. You then enter the Peak District National Park and the road heads south west on a straight section at 8% for 300 metres. If the wind is blowing, as it often does up here, it whips off the hillside and makes this section doubly hard. Stick with it as there is some slight shelter as you turn left across the hillside with gratifying views back towards Holmfirth which is now far below.

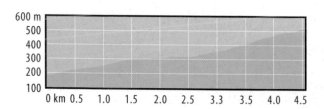

A right-hand bend initiates the final ¾ mile (1.2 kilometres), which the council have kindly marked on the road. In fact they have done this every ¼ mile since leaving Holme village, so you are always acutely aware of how much longer you have to suffer. The ascent fluctuates between 10% and 12% from now on, but it feels much harder. The road can feel like glue, but now the transmitter mast at the summit is very close as it towers imposingly above, whilst the slope to the left drops to Yateholme Reservoir. This diverse scene is stimulating, not least with the road ahead curving towards the summit. The sightseers already there slowly get closer until you eventually reach the summit car park, then a sign marking the top. This truly classic climb is now complete, but ahead is a superb descent to Woodhead from where you could ride over to Glossop and sample some other great Peak District climbs.

PROFESSIONAL RACING ON HOLME MOSS

Holme Moss has been a key ingredient in some of the biggest and best races ever staged in the UK. It was the scene of Stage 2 of the 1988 Kellogg's Tour of Britain from York to Manchester when riders were taken over Shibden Wall on the way to 'The Moss'. That day, Chris Walker of the Raleigh Banana team led a chasing peleton on the climb with Mike Doyle and Robert Millar in the bunch. Stephen Roche was also there in the World Champions jersey rebuilding form following a knee injury.

Holme Moss was also part of the Wincanton Classic in 1992: it formed Round 7 of the season-long World Cup competition. The World Cup also included the monuments of Milan San Remo, the Tour of Flanders and Liège–Bastogne–Liège so this UK round was a major international race. The stage, starting and finishing in Leeds, would take the riders 147 miles via Ilkley, Keighley and Oxenhope before taking in Holme Moss twice. This climb would therefore be crucial in determining the winner on the day.

Keighley's Dave Rayner attacked after Ilkley establishing an early lead but then began to suffer due to illness later on. However, on the first ascent of Holme Moss a small group of important riders, including Alex Zülle, made their first move, establishing a good lead. Behind them, the Z team and Festina were chasing with Kelly in tow. However, Zülle was setting an infernal pace, leading all the way to the summit establishing a one-minute lead. Behind, the World Cup leader at the time, Olaf Ludwig, was suffering at the back of the main bunch. This was to be a crucial point of the race.

Huge crowds covered Holme Moss on the day with Sean Kelly now leading a chase group of 40–50 riders. The key selection in the lead group included Argentin, Ghirotto, Chiappucci, Alcalá, Sunderland, Jalabert, Decker and Rooks and the winner would now come from here. By the second ascent of Holme Moss, Argentin and Chiappucci set a fierce tempo in an attempt to break the will of some in the group and by the summit the lead was now two minutes. Unsurprisingly, given his earlier efforts, Zülle began to fade but 31 other riders abandoned even before the second ascent.

With 22 miles left on the road back to Leeds, the attacks began, with Ghirotto lighting the touch paper. He was later joined by Jalabert with the rest left to chase. Jalabert had the pedigree and was the favourite to win. However, after 6 hours and 21 minutes in the saddle including two ascents of Holme Moss, the form book meant very little. Indeed, Ghirotto attacked and found no response from a cramping Jalabert. Holme Moss made a huge mark on the professional peleton in the 1980s and 1990s, being a key component in selecting the strongest riders within a race. Indeed, fewer than half the field reached the finish line in the 1992 Wincanton Classic.

6. JAWBONE HILL

Difficulty	●●●●●●◑○○○
Distance	1.8km
Av. Gradient	9.2%
Max. Gradient	15%
Height Gain	162m
Start Point	Oughtbridge, Station Lane off junction with A6102 GR: 307934 (OS Landranger: 110)
Local Cafés	Le Petit Café, 1a Church Street, Ecclesfield, Sheffield S35 9WE ☎ 07817 253858

It's a struggle to reach the top, and unfortunately it can be busy with commuter traffic at peak times, but Jawbone Hill is still worth the effort because the views of this green, hilly city from the summit are jaw-dropping. The ascent begins in the Sheffield suburb of Oughtibridge, heading eastward past a public park then climbing quickly through the edge of the residential area. The first 300 metres averages around 11% and involves the negotiation of a few speed bumps along the way. It's a strenuous introduction but as the road is squeezed at a bridge over the railway, the slope becomes steeper at

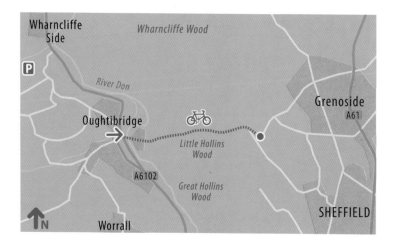

15% and continues for long enough to make it hurt. Suddenly the scene is more rustic although there are a few small industrial buildings at the side of the road. There is also a drive on the left that takes you into Wharncliffe Woods (where downhill mountain bike legend Steve Peat learned his trade). There are a number of great trails for all abilities around this forest if you prefer fat tyre cycling. However, back on the tarmac, the gradient fluctuates around 11% for 400 metres until you leave the shelter of the last few trees and houses.

The summit ridge of Birley Edge can now be seen on the horizon and the slope is much easier for a minute or so, but then ramps up briefly to 13% before becoming more consistent at around 8%. Ahead you can see the road bending right which takes you on to the final 200 metres rise to the top. It becomes steeper as you ascend and reaches around 12% just before the crest where a sharp and narrow left-hand bend immediately flattens out and allows you to recuperate. On this bend, beware of traffic, but if you can cross safely to the opposite side of the road there is a viewpoint where you can look out over Sheffield.

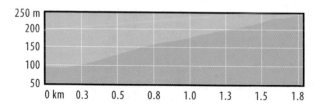

7. JENKIN ROAD

Difficulty	⬤⬤⬤⬤⬤⬤⬤◗○○
Distance	0.8km
Av. Gradient	11.2%
Max. Gradient	30%
Height Gain	94m
Start Point	Wincobank: South-eastern end of Jenkin Road at junction with B6082. GR: 386908 (OS Landranger 110)
Local Cafés	Costa Coffee, Princess Works, 10 Brightside Lane, Sheffield S9 3YE ☎ 01298 84838

Jenkin Road has a reputation outside cycling because new drivers and motorists lacking confidence in their hill starts would seek an alternative route from the valley below. It's a well-known road in the North East of Sheffield turning off the B6082 and up the steep side of the Don Valley to Wincobank. This is the home of Brendan Ingle's famous boxing gym and many champion fighters including Johnny Nelson and Herol 'Bomber' Graham. Accordingly, this climb requires tenacity and the ability to recover from a near knock-out blow. If ever there was an ascent for the 'puncheur', or the cyclist

accomplished in short and steep climbs, this is it.

The climb is very steep for the opening round with a gradient in double figures over the first 200 metres straight. If there was any doubt that you are in a real battle with gravity at this stage, a glance at the brick walls by the pavement show the

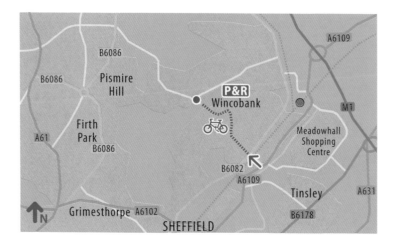

harsh incline. The slope reaches a sustained 14%, yet up ahead things are about to take a serious turn for the vertical.

The junction with Jenkin Drive on the left marks the start of a 200 metres segment that rivals the brutality of any other climb in the region. The slope rears up to 30% on a left-hand bend where handrails are provided for walkers to aid their passage. It's here that Jenkin Road tries to defeat you with a hurtful attack. Progress becomes agonisingly slow, but you must sustain the huge effort and fix on the horizon ahead where a further left-hand bend leads to a more forgiving segment at 14%.

Mercifully, albeit temporarily, the road levels out significantly to 5% for 50 metres as views towards the inner-city landscape of Don Valley can be glimpsed through the houses on the left. You now have Jenkin Road on the ropes because all that remains is a short 13% ramp to the summit. This final effort is insignificant compared to the fight so far, but it is important to keep going right to the final bell. At the end of this bout, you will have high regard for this arduous climb, but you will have earned respect in return as a rider bold enough to attempt it.

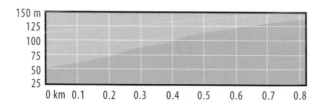

8. LONGSTONE EDGE

Difficulty	●●●●●●●○○○
Distance	2.2km
Av. Gradient	6.9%
Max. Gradient	17%
Height Gain	154m
Start Point	Great Longstone: Moor Road; junction with Main Street. GR: 197719 (OS Landranger 119)
Local Cafés	Yonderman Café, Wardlow Mires, Buxton SK17 8RW (A623) ☎ 01298 873056

Great Longstone sits in the heart of the Peak District amongst the limestone landscape that characterizes the 'White Peak' area.

The route to Longstone Edge is clearly signposted and leaves the village via a narrow lane amongst cottages and native trees. The gradient quickly increases to around 8% over the first sheltered straight section aiming directly at the steep hillside above. However, things soon get significantly tougher as the road slowly emerges into open fields and Longstone Edge is revealed. Over the next 400 metres the gradient is fairly sustained at around 13%, and requires a real effort to maintain your progress. It's as if you are heaving some of the valuable lead that is hidden beneath the surface here.

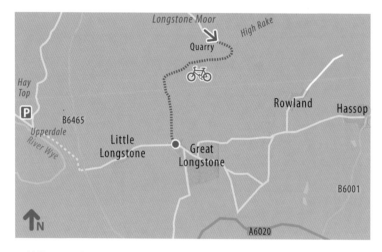

Half way to the summit, the road builders decided to cut across the slope rather than go straight ahead. Happily this means the second half of the climb becomes an overwhelmingly pleasurable experience as the tough component is now almost behind you. However, you must first navigate the 90-degree, right-hand bend that marks this halfway point and overcome the short, but nasty, 17% slope.

As you exit the bend and cross a cattle grid the road quickly levels and now heads in an easterly direction, which often means a helpful tail wind on this bare hillside. The slope stays close to 6% for the final 600 metres where lovely views open to the south, and the hillside to your right drops away beneath you. You ride amongst gorse and hawthorn whilst your upper body recovers and the legs now begin to spin a little more easily. This charming section of road is an absolute joy to ride.

Up ahead the road slowly bends left as you crest the summit. Signs of current mining activity become apparent here, but thankfully the major scars are hidden from view and it remains a satisfying pedal. The view now extends north to the gritstone landscape of the Dark Peak and the 600 metres summits of Mam Tor and Kinder Scout.

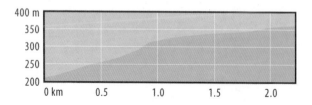

9. MAM NICK

Difficulty	●●●●●●●●○○
Distance	2.1km
Av. Gradient	9.8%
Max. Gradient	17%
Height Gain	202m
Start Point	Barber Booth: Edale Road Crossing with River Noe GR: 113847 (OS Landranger: 110)
Local Cafés	Penny Pot Café, Station Approach, Edale, Derbyshire S33 7ZA ☎ 01433 631111

Edale is a wild and imposing valley in the Dark Peak. At the head of the valley is a one-way exit provided by a road known as Mam Nick, which is justly feared by many club riders.

Shortly after passing Edale village a left-hand bend takes you on to the ascent where a sign accurately indicates a 16% incline. The surface is pretty poor for a short distance but it soon improves and is reasonable for the remainder of the climb. Over the first 400 metres the gradient is steep at 9%, but fairly constant in the shelter of hawthorn, as the slopes of Rushup Edge dominate the horizon ahead. The road bends left bringing a relatively pleasant stretch where the gradient hovers around 7% and magnificent views down Edale valley can be enjoyed. The summit can now also be seen for the first

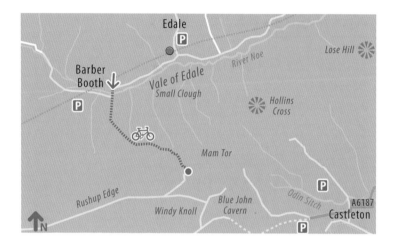

time – dauntingly high above. Try to keep spinning your lightest gear here because the second third of the climb is certainly where you will need to make the greatest effort.

There is a momentary flat period as the road bends left, taking you onto a weaving steep section where you are forced in and out of the saddle. The gradient is really challenging for the first time since the start, reaching around 17% at its hardest over a 400 metres stretch. The tarmac surface rolls over bumps, subtly altering the incline by 1–2% – just enough to slow your cadence or force a gear change if you have any left. There are also sections where small land slippages have created off-camber edges to the road, so line choice is important.

The road rises up again almost straight away towards 17%. This is the final, very tough section and the top brings the final twisting route amongst hillocks caused by landslips. Progress is still not easy as the road pitches up and down between 6% and 12%, but it doesn't rise too dramatically through the unusual landscape here. Keep pushing and you soon find yourself at the top, travelling through the narrow cutting between Mam Tor and Rushup Edge that seemed so far above a few minutes before.

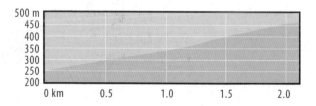

10. MONSAL HEAD

Difficulty	●●●●●●●○○○
Distance	0.6km
Av. Gradient	10.3%
Max. Gradient	18%
Height Gain	60m
Start Point	Monsal Dale: small layby on left of the lane GR: 182719 (OS Landranger 119)
Local Cafés	Hobb's Café, Monsal Head, Great Longstone, Bakewell DE45 1NL ☎ 01629 640346

The climb to Monsal Head is a stunning cycling ascent that stands out as a true classic despite being in the close company of many other superb climbs. Monsal has a story and the surroundings to make it a 'must do' for the cyclist aiming to experience a classic Peak District climb. It is admittedly very short at only 600 metres, but it is also very

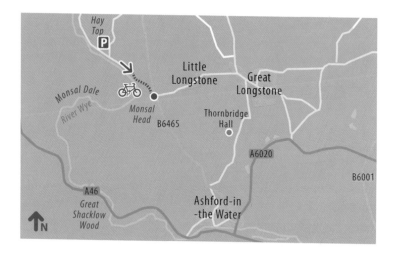

sweet. This stems partly from its place as a hill climb race venue since 1930 where many local legends including Malcolm Elliott, Chris Walker and Tom Simpson have raced. The backdrop is also about as beautiful as you will find anywhere in the Peak District. Monsal is a place to linger and absorb the ambience of this ancient geological masterpiece.

You begin on an enchanting lane down in Monsal Dale, which runs parallel to the gently flowing River Wye. As you pedal along, you will see the summit café high above on the skyline, but it's calm and tranquil down here under the tight protection of the steep slopes of Monsal Valley. However, the stillness of the flat valley road transforms quickly into a steep ascent where you are carried upward at a momentum-sapping rate on a slope reaching 18% by the end of the first 300 metres. The closeness of the trees offers protection from the elements, yet this can also mean the road is damp and slippery in places. The gradient is fairly constant and, although it is never super-steep, it doesn't drop below 15% at any point once you are immersed in the main slope.

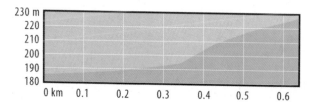

The tree cover slowly but surely dissipates as you climb skyward, as if you are emerging from a tunnel, with the daylight bursting through the gap ahead. A sign on the left indicates the final surge at 15% towards the terraced arena leading to the summit. It's time to find an extra gear if you can for the final effort, which culminates with a sharp left-hand bend and relief for throbbing thigh muscles.

A short roll around the corner offers the opportunity to clear the lactate, but the full Monsal experience should include a return to the crest of the climb. Here you can observe the breathtaking vista below towards the ancient Monsal Dale and Headstone Viaduct, built to carry local rail passengers in the late nineteenth and early twentieth century (a picturesque train line used to exist here but it was closed in 1959). It's also an opportunity to reflect on the many great riders who have fought gravity within this classic cycling venue. Here at Monsal Head you can experience the same climb that so many cycling heroes have raced.

MONSAL HILL CLIMB RACE

Monsal has been used as a venue for a hill climb competition since 1930 when a few friends rode out to race each other on what was then an un-metalled road. Eighty years later, enjoying a renaissance under the leadership of Marc Etches and Sheffrec CC, the race attracted a strong field including local legend Russell Downing as favourite. Downing, riding in Team Sky colours, was in a determined frame of mind, aiming to beat the long-standing course record of his friend and mentor, Malcolm Elliott.

The weather on the early October day was fairly cool and overcast with only light winds. Downing was now at the height of his powers as a cyclist, having won a contract with Team Sky in 2009. He then performed admirably during 2010, winning Stage 2 of the Criterium International and the Tour de Wallonie overall. The scene was set for an enthralling afternoon with high hopes of witnessing Elliott's record of 1 minute 14.2 seconds fall. This was especially so considering Downing was a three-times previous winner. He had come closer than anyone to the 1981 record, as a 25-year-old, with 1 minute 18.3 seconds.

Regardless of the weather conditions in 1981, Elliott's record time stood as an astonishing ride given the technology available at the time and his tender age of 20 – well before his peak. Many considered the record unbeatable. Nevertheless, the tension grew to a crescendo that afternoon as 119 riders attempted to re-write their own personal records before the big moment at 1pm. The expectation was now palpable in the crowd of several hundred spectators waiting on the terraced upper Monsal slope.

Malcolm Elliott himself was present as guest of honour for this eightieth anniversary race and reportedly had a bet on the outcome with Downing. Hill climbs tend to have a pleasant mix of serious competition mixed with that end-of-season frivolity. By 1pm the former was clearly foremost in Downing's mind as he appeared on the steepest final section of Monsal amongst the cheering crowd. Although moving noticeably quicker than previous riders, he appeared to be labouring under the 46/18 gear ratio he believed was necessary to beat the record. The crowd cheered with all their might, but Elliott's wry smile at the finish gave away the outcome before the official time was announced. 1 minute 20.5 seconds was well outside the record on this occasion but was good enough to win the race, whilst cementing Elliott's place as a bona fide hero of Monsal Hill climb.

OPPOSITE: Malcolm Elliott on Monsal. (Photo courtesy of Malcolm Elliott)

II. PEA ROYD LANE

Difficulty	●●●●●●●●●○
Distance	1.1km
Av. Gradient	12.7%
Max. Gradient	18%
Height Gain	146m
Start Point	Stocksbridge: Hunshelf Road after mini-roundabout through steelworks. GR: 182719 (OS Landranger 110)
Local Cafés	Works Lunchbox Café, 2 Hunshelf Road, Stocksbridge, Sheffield S36 2BU (at foot of climb) ☎ 0114 288 3391

To the north of Sheffield, in the satellite town of Stocksbridge, you will find one of the toughest of all British climbs. It has been used for hill climb competitions for some time and even hosted the national championships in 2009. Pea Royd Lane is a real beast with three sections of ferociously steep tarmac, and these steep sections are interspersed with slopes that are only marginally easier. This is a climb that requires a hard core of steel in order to reach the top.

The opening 200 metres climb at around 10–12%, followed by a fairly easy stretch of 100 metres around 5% within rather ugly metal fencing and a

(Photo: Dawn Chetwynd)

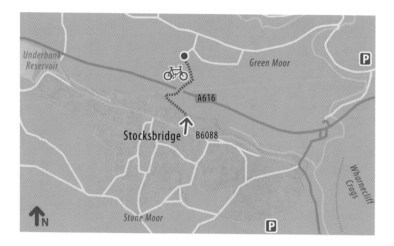

poor road surface that continues for much of the ascent. Towards the end of this section you will notice a transition to a more natural and pleasing view of trees.

A 90-degree right turn takes you onto Pea Royd Lane itself where the first ferocious part of the climb appears taking you rapidly upward at 18% for 200 metres of real suffering. The slope does relent as you cross the bridge over the A616, but it's not enough to give you a meaningful recovery. Moreover you are now amongst a more exposed agricultural landscape. The remaining hillside can now be seen in its full glory with Pea Royd Lane climbing perpendicularly then cutting left to avoid the near-vertical Hunshelf Bank.

The second gruelling section begins with a quickly inclining slope that reaches 18% again and remains so through a right-hand curve, then a brutal left-hand hairpin, which you should take as wide as traffic allows. It's another 200 metres of exhausting climbing which briefly relents then takes you back to an 18% slope for a further 50 metres. The remaining 100 metres carry you upward at around 10% with a short but steep finale until you finally reach Green Moor.

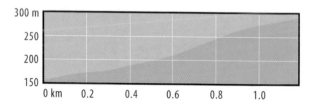

12. PYM CHAIR

Difficulty	●●●●●●●●◐○
Distance	1.5km
Av. Gradient	11%
Max. Gradient	20%
Height Gain	167m
Start Point	Hooleyhey Lane crossing with Todd Brook GR: 983763 (OS Landranger: 118)
Local Cafés	Yellow Teapot Café, Smith Lane, Rainow, Macclesfield SK10 5XJ ☎ 01625 574878

The Goyt Valley is a magnet for cyclists and other outdoor enthusiasts. Pym Chair from the west is arguably the best climb in the vicinity because it provides a tough culmination to a number of strength-sapping approaches, most notably Blaze Hill.

The prelude to the climb involves a pleasant descent towards Todd Brook after which the lane turns northward and begins to lift you at around 10% towards the summit some 1.5 kilometres away. A brief levelling, as you pass the beautifully situated Jenkin Chapel, is the place to prepare for lift off because the road becomes much steeper now. Over the next few minutes you are given no option but to pedal further and deeper into your reserves with almost no escape until the top.

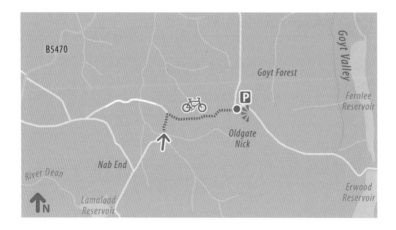

The first stretch is smooth, in the tyre tracks of vehicles, until you reach a short ramp at 17%, which briefly flattens but goes up again quickly to 19%. You will experience that inescapable heaving on the pedals associated with super-steep climbs, but after this there is a short stretch where the gradient is more forgiving. However, it is not enough to allow a good recovery (assuming you resist the temptation to stop for a breather). Things now get increasingly demanding as you pass Pym Chair Farm. It's difficult to settle into a rhythm on this climb with several changes in pitch. This late segment is no exception as another brief levelling is followed by a very steep left-hand bend.

You are now on the brutal 400-metre stretch to the summit, which is more sustained and never drops below 15%, but reaches 20%. Breathtaking, far-away views open to the left, but your attention is absorbed by the physical effort required to overcome the increasingly demanding slope. As you throw your bike side-to-side on this killer section you will be close to your limit, but up ahead the suffering is about to end. Once past the car park and cattle grid, unclip from the pedals and delay your descent for a while to take in the panorama.

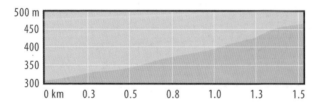

13. SCOTSMAN'S

Difficulty	●●●●●●●◑○○
Distance	3.4km
Av. Gradient	7.9%
Max. Gradient	16%
Height Gain	271m
Start Point	Hathersage: Scotsman's Pack Public House; junction of School Lane and Church Bank GR: 234817 (OS Landranger 110)
Local Cafés	Hathersage Pool Café, Oddfellows Road, Hathersage, Hope Valley S32 1DU ☎ 01433 651159

Heading east out of the northern Peak District you are spoilt for choice in terms of cycling climbs. The magnificent gritstone edge that dominates the eastern edge of High Peak provides the huge natural barrier that you must overcome. Several roads that climb this edge, although tempting to ride, are often busy with tourist traffic and

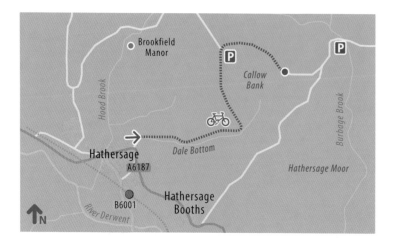

should be saved for quieter periods. One of the quieter routes leaves the Scotsman's Pack pub in Hathersage and climb for over 3 kilometres to the mighty Stanage Edge.

The climb begins on School Lane taking you past the Scotsman's Pack pub itself as you gently ascend past cottages and a babbling brook. There are few cars here compared with other routes and this early section serves as the perfect roll out, preparing you for the moment when the road kicks upward.

Enclosed in a steep-sided, sheltered valley, you climb steeply for around 400 metres. The road surface is good, but at 1 in 6, you really have to pedal strongly. It is a strangely satisfying climb. It's a challenge for sure, but not so severe that you have to revert to a primal survival mode, hung over the bars and gasping for breath. Nevertheless, once you reach a warning sign then a left-hand bend, the gradient eases to around 8% and remains so for just under a kilometre. The landscape now opens to gradually reveal the remainder of the climb.

As you draw near to Stanage Edge you pass a car park used primarily by adrenaline junkies to test their mettle on the legendary rock climbs above. The gradient relents

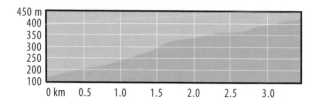

allowing a freewheel before the final slope which is certainly enough to put you back into the red if you push hard, although the incline doesn't go above 10%. It's a good opportunity to look right and take in one of the most the spectacular High Peak views. It's no wonder Charlotte Brontë found inspiration for her classic novel Jane Eyre on these moors and at the sixteenth-century North Lees Hall nestled in the valley below.

The road gradually eases as you pass a bench on the left. You might be tempted to jump off the bike to soak up the view, but it's also a chance to finish strongly if you can, as you finally draw level with the cliff edge. Unclip at the top instead and admire the view, which extends over to Higger Tor and Carl Wark where an Iron Age hill fort once existed. Then, if you have the time, consider turning right at the T-junction ahead, which takes you on the exhilarating descent of 'Fiddlers Elbow' back to Hathersage.

THE FLYING SCOTSMAN ON SCOTSMAN'S

On an average day the Scotsman's Climb is a fairly quiet road used mainly by villagers and rock climbers on their way to Stanage Edge. However, 2 August 1990 was certainly no average day as some of the world's greatest cyclists would pass through during Stage 3 of the Kellogg's Tour of Britain. A heatwave had hit the UK with temperatures reaching 36° as the peleton rode from Birmingham to Sheffield over 96 miles (154 kilometres). Hundreds of excited spectators lined the road awaiting the arrival of champion riders such as Stephen Roche, Maurizio Fondriest and Phil Anderson. Yet it was Robert Millar, the climbing superstar of the Tour de France, whom the crowd were perhaps most eager to see in action.

The stage was ideal for Millar's primary weapon of choice with relentless climbing within the final miles through the Peak District. Millar was riding for the legendary 'Z team' with whom Greg LeMond had recently won his third Tour de France. Millar had promised to attack prior to the stage and he was true to his word, establishing a significant lead over the peleton and Yellow Jersey wearer, Laurent Jalabert. Millar had hopes of winning the stage and securing the race lead, but there was a fly in the ointment in the shape of Belgian rider Michel Dernies, who recognized the danger and chased Millar across the Peaks.

By the time Millar reached Scotsman's, named 'Hathersage Climb' in the race, he had been caught by Dernies. Both rode up the climb 70 seconds ahead of the next chasing rider. The crowd on the upper slopes of the climb could see the riders approaching from on far and they were ecstatic to see Millar in the lead. A wall of sound met Millar as he sped past, resplendent in the best climber's jersey, based on the polka dots of the equivalent Tour de France jersey but with red Ks instead of spots. The peleton arrived a few minutes later with photos showing cyclists, including local Chris Walker, riding up the climb drinking 2-litre bottles of water passed to them by spectators.

The lead duo rode to the finish in Sheffield where they would complete on a city centre circuit. They arrived 2 minutes ahead of a ten-man chasing group including Maurizio Fondriest. Elliott, Anderson, Roche and Jalabert were in a third group about 3 minutes behind. Millar had to beat Dernies to take the race lead and was in a strong position on his wheel approaching the final sprint. However, the chasing riders caught the front two, albeit a lap down, and swamped Millar leaving him no chance of attacking. It was a disappointing end to a fascinating race but Millar had truly shown his class, as this legendary Scotsman flew up Scotsman's climb.

OPPOSITE: *Chris Walker on Scotsman's. (Photo: paphotos.co.uk)*

14. STAINBOROUGH

Difficulty	●●●●●●●◐○○
Distance	1km
Av. Gradient	9%
Max. Gradient	18%
Height Gain	89m
Start Point	Stainborough: Lowe Lane (eastern end); left bend after junction with Gilroyd Lane GR: 323038 (OS Landranger 110)
Local Cafés	Wentworth Castle Tea Room, Wentworth Castle Gardens, Lowe Lane, Stainborough, Barnsley S75 3ET ☎ 01226 776040

In the vicinity of Barnsley, within the quiet rolling lanes between the hills of the Peak District and the flatlands of East Yorkshire there is a great deal of tough cycling country. Inside this area is a splendid climb that passes one of the most commanding historical houses in Britain: Stainborough Lowe Lane takes you alongside the Grade 1 listed Wentworth Castle. More crucially, Stainborough Lowe Lane is a road widely used to test a rider's form because there is no hiding place on this consistently steep climb.

The beginning is steep enough at 10% as you leave the scattering of houses that make up Stainborough village, and the road surface is pitted and uneven. This relatively forgiving introductory gradient becomes really severe as you enter the woodland and

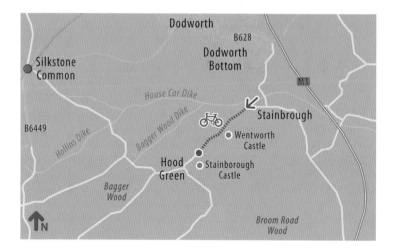

the road steepens to 18% for 100 metres, and then relents slightly. The term 'relent' is used in relative terms because over the next interminable 200 metres the slope maintains 15% until you reach the entrance to the Northern College. You hit the anaerobic threshold early on in this climb and you are forced to remain above it for a drawn-out period.

During this unremitting section it is worth remembering that one of the hardest cyclists known to modern man has used this climb many times to hone his fitness. Ex-pro Wayne Randle, from the nearby mining village of Cudworth, used this ascent to hone his legs into the killer limbs that gave him the moniker 'Wayne the Train'.

After this strenuous section, the slope does lessen for a very short interlude before it returns to 13% for a brief but potentially morale-breaking period. Thankfully the finale eases significantly to 4% where you pass a milestone built into the stone wall and almost hidden from view. At this point you will be well cooked, but you will have ridden a climb endorsed by Randle.

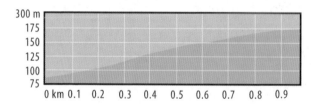

15. WINNATS PASS

Difficulty	⦿⦿⦿⦿⦿⦿⦿⦿⦿⦿
Distance	1.5km
Av. Gradient	12.1%
Max. Gradient	21%
Height Gain	180m
Start Point	Castleton: A6187 turn off left to Arthurs Way/ Winnats Road. GR: 144828 (OS Landranger 110)
Local Cafés	Three Roofs Café, The Island, Castleton, Hope Valley, Derbyshire S33 8WN ☎ 01433 620533

There are few climbs to match the severity of Winnats Pass. As you ride further and further up the slope, you become steadily but increasingly starved of oxygen with absolutely no respite. Its grip on your breathing becomes tighter and tighter as the road rears upward in its unrelenting climb towards the Shivering Mountain of Mam Tor.

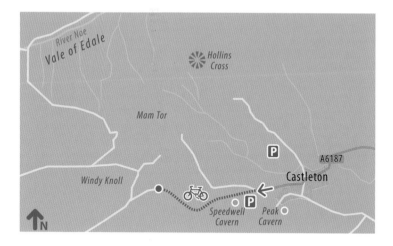

The climb starts just outside the attractive village of Castleton and ascends almost 200 metres in just over a kilometre. There is nowhere to hide here – no option other than to dig in and tough it out with one of the cruellest climbs anywhere in the country.

The ride from Castleton is an opportunity to take in the view upwards to Mam Tor and the Great Ridge before the left-hand turn takes you on the initial slope towards the tourist honey-pot of Blue John caverns. This straight 500-metre section appears innocuous enough because of the contrast between the main climb that you can now see cut into the chasm ahead. However, the slow pace and selection of the easiest gears reveals that this is already a significant incline, reaching 13%. A cattle grid marks the point where you leave the sanctuary of the caverns and enter the clutches of the main climb.

The scenery around you is now truly magnificent with cliffs and limestone out-crops almost 150 metres above. Unfortunately it's from here that the gradient becomes increasingly severe and unforgiving so you may not notice the grandeur. The

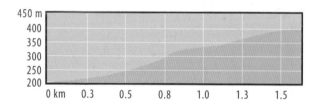

temptation is already to grit your teeth, sink your head and grind it out. However, you must keep focused and keep an eye on loose sheep or vehicles struggling with the vertiginous slope. Over 1 kilometre the gradient steadily increases from 13% to beyond 20%. It makes this ascent progressively more suffocating, especially when combined with the head wind that often funnels down the gorge.

By the final third of this climb, legs and lungs will be on fire. The upper body also takes a severe beating as you pull hard on the handlebars and engage your core abdominal muscles. This final section feels interminable as the gradient is sustained at around 20% for far too long. But the end is now in sight as the steep sides of the pass give way and a cattle grid marks the end of the most gruelling section of the climb. The final 400 metres fluctuate around 7% so there is an opportunity to return to the saddle and grind out the remaining section until you reach a T-junction. Turn right here to head towards Mam Tor or left towards Peak Forest, but rest assured that whichever direction you choose, you will be recovering for some time to come.

THE NATURE OF BRITISH HILL CLIMBS

Hills in Britain are the no-nonsense, straight-talking cousins of the more deliberate and considered climbs found on the continent. They are often much shorter in length compared to the mammoth ascents found in European mountains used for famous professional cycling races. However, they are often much steeper, reaching gradients in excess of 20% for sustained periods. A very large proportion of these climbs are to be found around the Pennine hills, known as the spine of England, which is largely within the Peak District and Yorkshire.

The fitness and mental approach required when climbing British hills is therefore quite different from that required when climbing Alpe d'Huez or Mont Ventoux, for example. On the latter you will be climbing for over an hour at a fairly consistent average, perhaps around 9%. As such you will be required to maintain a steady and sustainable pace. With correct gearing and reasonably good fitness you can stay just below your anaerobic threshold and utilize your fat stores to provide some of the energy needed for the ascent. From a mental perspective Alpine climbs are extremely daunting as you need to prepare yourself for being close to your limit for a prolonged period.

British climbs require a much more aggressive mentality in comparison. Regardless of gearing used, the brutal gradients and rough tarmac often require you to cross the red line into your anaerobic zone and you will need the capacity and determination to stay there for several minutes. The physical discomfort experienced in British climbs is far more acute, but it is thankfully short-lived. However, you are likely to have to repeat the experience several times on an average ride around the Peak District or Yorkshire.

16. CRAGG VALE

Difficulty	⬤⬤⬤⬤⬤◖○○○○
Distance	8.6km
Av. Gradient	3.4%
Max. Gradient	8%
Height Gain	296m
Start Point	Mytholmroyd: B6138 (Cragg Road), Blue Cragg Vale sign. GR: 011258 (OS Landranger 104)
Local Cafés	The Robin Hood Inn, Cragg Vale, Hebden Bridge HX7 5SQ ☎ 01422 885899

Cragg Vale is not a steep climb, but due to its continuous nature you will find this a stern test of muscular endurance. The initial slope is very gentle but as you pass a sign welcoming you to Cragg Vale, the road steepens to 5%, which represents the gradient for much of the first half. There are white lines marked on the road counting down the remaining kilometres as you ascend and you can use these as targets, so find your rhythm and settle in for the long haul.

Spinning past the colourful hanging baskets clinging to wrought iron fencing, there is the impression that the locals take pride in their community. It's clear to see why within this first 3-kilometre stretch, with glimpses of the attractive valley and hillside.

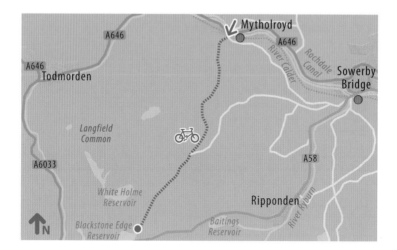

The latter gives daunting indication of the height yet to be climbed whilst the swirling winds here make it slightly more challenging to calculate your effort.

After a few twists and turns you begin to rise above the treeline and the incline rises to 8%. This is the most strenuous section as you exit the village with 4 kilometres remaining. You are now really exposed to the wind amongst the wild heather moorland that now provides the backdrop for the second half of the climb. It's pretty tough here but the grade does soon relent.

The masts on the horizon now provide a focus point as the kilometre markers are ticked off one by one. The road does not get steeper than 3% for the second half so progress becomes swifter. Indeed, it's almost flat as you ride the final kilometre and a solid white line marks the summit where you can roll through and reflect on your latest achievement. A junction by Blackstone Reservoir offers you the option of riding to Halifax or Rochdale. However, you should turn around to experience the thrill of the longest continuous descent in England.

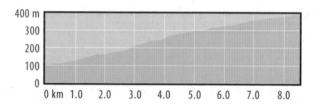

17. HALIFAX LANE

Difficulty	⬤⬤⬤⬤⬤⬤⬤⬤◯
Distance	1.6km
Av. Gradient	11%
Max. Gradient	21%
Height Gain	178m
Start Point	Luddenham: Halifax Lane at junction with High Street. GR: 042260 (OS Landranger 104)
Local Cafés	Milly's Café, Grange Dene, Mytholmroyd, Hebden Bridge HX7 5LL ☎ 01422 883504

The former textile town of Luddenden in Calderdale was once a hub of several pack-horse routes between larger towns in the area. One of these routes, Halifax Lane, provides this particular challenge. After a short descent down High Street (signposted 'unsuitable for HGVs') there is a sharp right turn onto Halifax Lane, which rises very steeply as you pass a playground and some post-war housing. The slope reaches 20% past some older terraced houses built from local sandstone along a very smooth stretch of tarmac. The gradient is still 16% as you reach a right-hand bend, but it becomes extremely steep again, reaching 20% over 100 metres. The view over the valley opens at this point and fortunately the gradient relents so that you can look around a little.

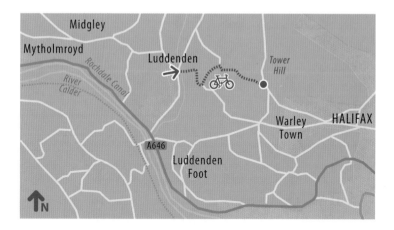

The road becomes steeper once again as you take the left-hand bend on Birch Lane where you may notice a pleasant smell of pine needles in the air. You will certainly be inhaling hard because the gradient touches 21% briefly before levelling to 10% for a while. The views are now to the left and are sensational, highlighting the industrial nature of the village. You are now climbing on a hillside road with a steep drop. This is a fantastic climb: it is hard but it is a real pleasure to ride at the same time. You feel rewarded and stimulated as you ascend.

It remains hard but then as you approach a right-hand bend the gradient approaches insanity yet again and is fairly sustained – you will really have to heave the pedals around. As you reach the bend the slope is still at 17% but it is vital you take a wide approach because the inside is close to vertical. The view is now even more tremendous than before with greater depth across the Calderdale region. The tough stuff is almost at an end but a right turn onto Raw End Road takes you once more to 17% before it levels to a more sustainable incline as you enter the open farmland. For the final 300 metres you might be able to remain seated until you reach the summit where there is a T-junction with Heath Hill Road.

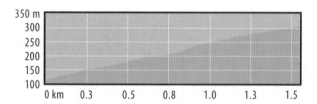

18. ILKLEY MOOR

Difficulty	●●●●●●●○○
Distance	1.7km
Av. Gradient	10.6%
Max. Gradient	19%
Height Gain	179m
Start Point	Ilkley: Wells Road junction with B6382 Station Road GR: 117475 (OS Landranger 104)
Local Cafés	Smooth Café, 14–16 Wells Road, Ilkley LS29 9JD ☎ 01943 600064

There are two climbs from the town heading up to Ilkley Moor. The eastern ascent carries you toward the Cow and Calf rocks and was part of the Leeds Classic and Tour of Britain cycling races. However, this ascent is busy with traffic and a quieter, more challenging alternative lies slightly to the west. This climb finishes at a dead end, but it is still well worth the effort.

The climb begins on Wells Road, which carries you steeply for 200 metres, but this

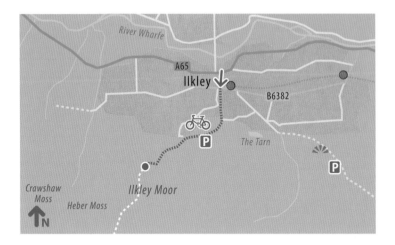

residential one-way boulevard offers no major hurdle at this stage. You then reach a more comfortable section where you pass the Millennium Maze celebrating the town's links with Charles Darwin who once stayed here to take advantage of the Spa. The famous Ilkley Moor now appears to the left with delightfully undulating gorse, bracken and heather providing a pleasing transition from the urban to rural landscape. The road here flattens for 100 metres before a left-hand bend changes the ambience significantly. The road is about to become very steep and the ride changes from a sightseeing venture to a genuine challenge.

The gradient increases towards 17% before reaching a stone bridge where tourists linger. The temptation is to join them but a more powerful emotion drives you onward towards the obviously steep ramp ahead. The next left-hand bend takes you on to a much rougher surface and onto the most sustained and brutal part of the climb. This is the point of no return where you reach a slope that fluctuates between 16% and 19% over 300 metres. There is no option but to rise from the saddle and heave on the bars as the road becomes an un-metalled track.

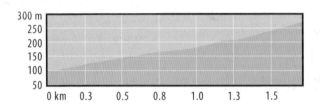

19. JACKSON BRIDGE

Difficulty	●●●●●●●●○○
Distance	1.6km
Av. Gradient	9.9%
Max. Gradient	20%
Height Gain	159m
Start Point	Jackson Bridge: turn off A616 onto South View GR: 166075 (OS Landranger 110)
Local Cafés	Brooklands Nurseries & Coffee Shop, Scholes, Holmfirth HD9 1UJ ☎ 01484 683891

The climb begins steadily when you turn off the main A616 on to South View and ride past a few bungalows. Shortly afterwards you will turn left on to Staley Royd Lane where the road becomes steeper towards 12% and this is where the first part

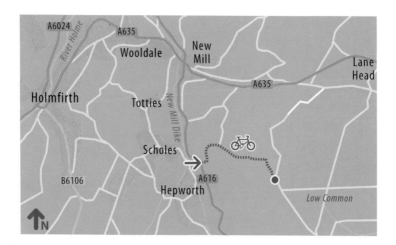

of the climb now becomes more extreme and direct. After a hairpin right-hand bend the gradient kicks up to 20% forcing you over the bars and into the oxygen debt, but kindly this is short-lived and the slope decreases to around 7% as you pass a clutch of houses. The views to Holmfirth and over Kirklees in the north west are superb and can be enjoyed for a few moments, but after a curve to the right where the gradient slowly reaches 16%, and re-mains so for a lung-busting period.

There is a slight easing up where the view over to the wild hillside of Holme Moss is spectacular. A bench is strategically positioned to make the most of the vista. Soon after this point the gradient increases again to 14% and you sense the need to push harder and harder on the pedals and your reserves are squeezed further until a very small downhill and 90-degree bend taking you toward the final slope.

There are now only a few hundred meters remaining, beginning at 11% allowing you to ride at a more rhythmic cadence. However, toward the hilltop this climb doggedly refuses to relent completely as it reaches 15% at the summit and the junction with Intake Lane.

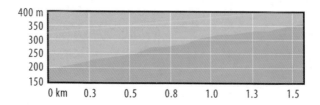

20. MEAL HILL

Difficulty	⦿⦿⦿⦿⦿⦿⦿◐○○
Distance	1km
Av. Gradient	12%
Max. Gradient	21%
Height Gain	125m
Start Point	Slaithwaite: Meal Hill Lane (southern end) at junction with Royd Street. GR: 079143 (OS Landranger 110)
Local Cafés	Bolster Moor Café and Farm Shop, Harden Road Farm, 1a Bolster Moor Road, Golcar, Huddersfield HD7 4JU ☎ 01484 648271

If you were to analyse the profile of an average ride around the Colne Valley, south west of Huddersfield, it would resemble a row of shark's teeth. A quick look at a map reveals a dense network of lanes north and south of the river, almost all of which have a chevron indicating a steep slope. Meal Hill Lane, north of Slaithwaite, is no exception and involves a continuously difficult slope with a really nasty 200 metres at the end.

The climb begins with a ride past Slaithwaite train station taking you to Meal Hill

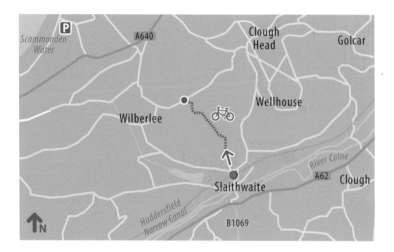

Lane where there is an easy start (6%) for 200 metres through the periphery of the town. There is then a steep section reaching 14%, which skirts around the edge of a hillside overlooking a picturesque valley to your right.

The navigation of Meal Hill continues to be fairly steady for 100 metres at around 12% until a short, steep pitch past some farmhouses on the right. Here it reaches 17% then returns to the climb's standard gradient of around 12% for 200 metres. By now you are amongst the shelter of a deep cutting and the road surface is very good considering this is a minor lane. It's an enjoyable ride, but the final gorging on vertical height will begin around the next right-hand bend.

The slope kicks up to 18% and stays there for an intense 100 metres until you reach a tight left-hand bend. There is a chance for a very slight recovery over five pedal revolutions; then the road goes up to 18% again for the final 100 metres. Right at the end you have to push extremely hard as the slope squeezes beyond 20%, but it is only temporary and you reach a junction where you can immediately stop pedalling.

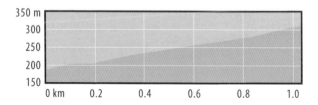

21. MYTHOLM STEEPS

Difficulty	⊘⊘⊘⊘⊘⊘⊘⊘⊘◖
Distance	1.6km
Av. Gradient	12%
Max. Gradient	28%
Height Gain	193m
Start Point	Hebden Bridge/Mytholm: Church Lane; junction with A646. GR: 985273 (OS Landranger 103)
Local Cafés	Watergate Tearooms, 9 Bridge Gate, Hebden Bridge, Halifax HX7 8EX ☎ 01422 842978

There are enough climbs around Hebden Bridge and Calderdale to write a separate chapter for the area, but there is one brute that stands out from the crowd: Mytholm Steeps. The climb begins just outside Hebden Bridge. As you exit the town and head west towards Todmorden, you turn onto Church Lane and begin climbing straight away on a 19% gradient with a broken surface on the left-hand side of the road. You then curve left past a chimney and there is a chance for minimal recovery before being sent upward again, but this time more steeply at 21%. The road becomes smoother by this point with only 200 metres completed, but the gradient remains at around 15%. There is nowhere to hide here, and it's at about this point where you may question your ability to reach the top or, more likely, question your sanity.

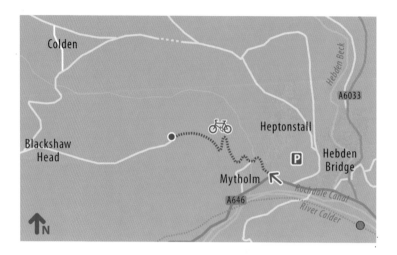

Happily there is a slightly easier section at 10% past a clutch of terraced houses where you enter Rawtonstall Wood, but then you return to the steep stuff yet again. First there is a 19% incline over a bumpy surface, then it touches 23% over a 100-metre section. It is energy-depleting and physically murderous, but there is a sense of enjoyment on this climb.

So far the climb has already been amongst the toughest Yorkshire has to offer, but the crux now appears before you. It's a scary vision when you are heaving the pedals over and you can clearly see the road ramping up even more steeply. There is no subtlety here as you reach 28% during a truly gruesome 100-metre period.

Thankfully, the climb gets much easier as the road bends left at a hairpin. You will notice how high you now are above the valley with steep wooded banks on your left. The remaining slopes take you from the woodland and onto the moors where the gradient fluctuates between 10% and 15%, but head winds might add to the difficulty.

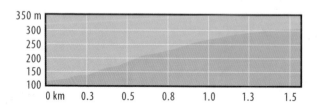

22. NORWOOD ROAD

Difficulty	⬤⬤⬤⬤⬤⬤◖○○○
Distance	1.8km
Av. Gradient	9.2%
Max. Gradient	20%
Height Gain	165m
Start Point	Bridge on B6451 crossing Lindley Wood Reservoir GR: 209499 (OS Landranger 104)
Local Cafés	Cock Pit Farm Tea Rooms, Moor Lane, Weston, Otley LS21 2HS ☎ 01943 464689

To get to Norwood Edge follow the B6451 north from Otley and after a short descent from Farnley to Lindley Wood reservoir you begin the climb. The opening is the steepest part of the climb, rising without delay to 14% then to 20% within the first 200 metres. It's a pretty extreme start to the climb and it gets you puffing exceptionally hard within the first few minutes. The surface is smooth but the gradient remains very strenuous for a further 200 metres becoming exposed to the wind as you ascend. The

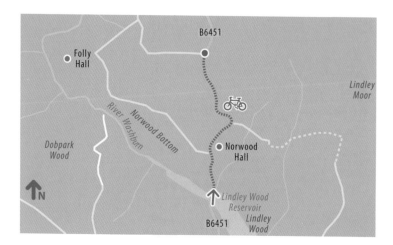

slope then increases again to 17% before yielding as you pedal around the right-hand curve. This opening half a kilometre should not be taken too lightly.

You then cycle up a steadily more forgiving slope that appears to traverse the hillside heading north east and climbing at around 7% for 400 metres. This is the time to catch your breath as you approach the halfway point of the climb. On the next sharp left-hand bend the gradient kicks up yet again to 13% then becomes a hard and sustained climb at around 10% as you become further exposed to the winds. If it's a westerly, which is most common, you will have a gluey crosswind to contend with, making this relatively tame gradient significantly more challenging. Some shelter is provided as you pass a small area of woodland on the left, but the road surface now becomes more bumpy and oppressive.

The final few hundred metres continues at around 8% and feels harder than you would expect until a definitive brow ahead and woodland track indicates the summit. The road then descends towards the classic road race circuit of Penny Pot Lane close to the historic spa town of Harrogate.

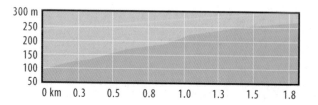

23. ROBIN HOOD CLIMB

Difficulty	●●●●●●●●○○
Distance	0.9km
Av. Gradient	13.6%
Max. Gradient	18%
Height Gain	122m
Start Point	Silsden: Holden Lane; Junction with Canal Lane and entrance to Howden Park Farm GR: 055453 (OS Landranger 104)
Local Cafés	Bilaluci Café, 55 Kirkgate, Keighley BD20 0AQ ☎ 01535 658273

Just outside Silsden in West Yorkshire is a climb that is recognized as one of the toughest climbs from the Airedale Valley. Starting from a quiet housing estate, there is an

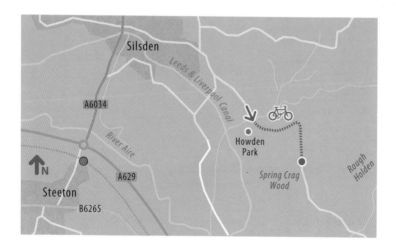

easy approach winding amongst hedgerows that offer some protection from wayward balls from Silsden Golf Course. After the twists and turns there is no doubt as to when the main climb begins. The road goes up viciously to 16% after a left turn and remains steep for 100 metres. The road is smooth, although there is the odd rough gravelly section, but nothing to slow progress further than the incline itself.

A respite period lasting about five pedal revolutions takes you to a second 100-metre steep stretch but this time the gradient reaches 18%. By this point your legs will be feeling the strain but there is only minimal reprieve again before you are taken on to a third, sustained pitch at 18%. It's a tortuous ascent whilst around you emerald green fields are now revealed.

A 90-degree right-hand bend brings a slightly easier segment with views across Airedale to the right. You can return to the saddle briefly but there is a sting in the tail because the final 150 metres takes you back towards 18%. Fortunately the 'killer kilometre' ends here and the slope relents significantly but the 'murder mile' has a short distance to go. It isn't flat but it is much easier.

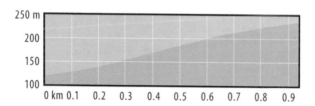

24. SHIBDEN WALL

Difficulty	⊙⊙⊙⊙⊙⊙⊙⊙⊙⊙
Distance	0.9km
Av. Gradient	15.2%
Max. Gradient	23%
Height Gain	133m
Start Point	Halifax/Northowram: Lee Lane junction with Simm Carr Lane; Bridge over Shibden Brook GR: 110274 (OS Landranger 104)
Local Cafés	Eight Sixteen Coffee, F Mill, Dean Clough, Halifax HX3 5AX ☎ 01422 331199

If you fancy experiencing the peculiar delights of cobbled climbing, but are unable to travel to Flanders for the classic ascents of the Muur-Kapelmuur or Paterberg, you could do worse than go to West Yorkshire and the Calderdale valley. There are several to choose from, but the most notorious is the Shibden Wall in Halifax.

The road itself is called 'Lee Lane' but following Stage 2 of the 1988 Kellogg's Tour of Britain it secured the name of 'Shibden Wall'. This is a cruelly steep ascent, but the cobbles, often gapped and uneven, make this an even sterner test of endurance.

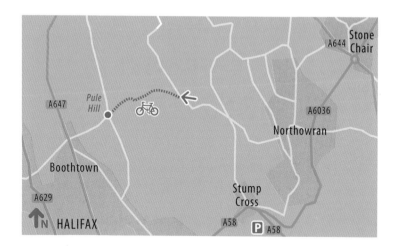

Follow Lee Lane up the slope where a 'I in 4' sign confirms the route and trees protect you from any winds. It's a tarmacked 16% at first, but the road levels out quickly to a more manageable, yet still strenuous, incline. Enjoy this introduction because the cobbles appear after 200 metres and the gradient cranks up to 23%.

The road remains ridiculously steep on a right-hand bend; then there is a switchback, where the stones become more uneven. Be careful not to get your front tyre lodged within the gaps. Getting started again on this sustained 20% slope is almost impossible. In 1988, even the strongest riders in the professional peleton were tempted to seek the refuge of the smoother footpath on the left, but if possible stay on the cobbles for optimal torment.

A right-hand bend brings houses into view and, following the briefest lull, the gradient kicks up yet again to 20% and the cobbles remain irregular. All your attention will be focused on choosing a route avoiding the gaps, but the summit will now be clearly in view. It's still steep and far enough away, but your motivation will be high and one last push will bring you to an immediate summit.

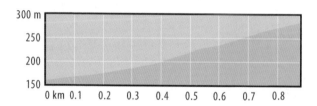

25. THWAITES BROW

Difficulty	⦿⦿⦿⦿⦿⦿⦿⦿⦿◖
Distance	1.2km
Av. Gradient	10.1%
Max. Gradient	20%
Height Gain	123m
Start Point	Keighley/Thwaites: start of cobbles on Thwaites Brow Road. GR: 076414 (OS Landranger 104)
Local Cafés	The Kitchen Café, 68 Haworth Road, Cross Roads, Keighley BD22 9DL ☎ 01535 647755

There is little fanfare on the approach to Thwaites Brow. Only the 'Unsuitable for HGVs' signpost gives away this climb's concealed location, but as soon as you hit the old cobbles you are are immediately pitched into a real struggle as the road kicks up to between 15% and 20%.

If the gradient wasn't enough to really test you, the cobbles here are broken and uneven, further depleting your energy. It also demands an acute route-finding ability to negotiate your path through the gaps.

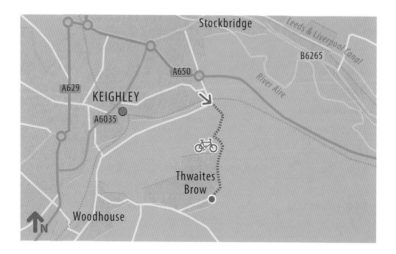

The steepness is pretty consistent on the first portion of the climb as the road bends right, then left amongst farmland. Then comes the steepest part of the ascent where the gradient surpasses 20% and the cobbles are at their most unforgiving. A right-hand turn then opens up towards a residential area and the steepness continues at 17%. There is a footpath on the right here, if you need it, but it only lasts for 100 metres or so. There is also the odd patch of tarmac, offering momentary relief from the intense vibration and concentration.

The briefest of levelling leads to further steepness as the road sweeps right, then left, then right again and to the top of the cobbled section. It is quite a relief as you are pitched back to the future and your wheels roll over the smooth tarmac. Your upper body will have taken a battering, but there is still more pedalling to do before you reach the summit of the full climb. It's fairly rolling, with a steep 100-metre section at 15%. Nonetheless, after a couple more minutes you will have the opportunity to finally pull in, realign your spine and check your bike is still in one piece.

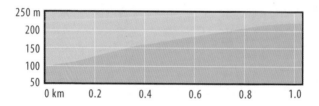

26. TROOPER LANE

Difficulty	◎◎◎◎◎◎◎◎◎◎
Distance	0.7km
Av. Gradient	19.1%
Max. Gradient	27%
Height Gain	137m
Start Point	Halifax: Siddal New Road/Swan Bank Lane junction; start of cobbles. GR: 098245 (OS Landranger 104)
Local Cafés	Eight Sixteen Coffee, F Mill, Dean Clough, Halifax HX3 5AX ☎ 01422 331199

Trooper Lane, just outside Halifax city centre, is perhaps the king of cobbled climbs in Yorkshire and will provide the optimum thrill for those excited by tradition or self-imposed suffering. You begin in East Halifax amongst light industrial units and Stoney Royd Cemetery. A turn onto the cobbled Swan Bank Lane marks the beginning of the ascent. You should be nervous at this point as the road shakes and ramps quickly

to 14%. After 50 metres you take a right turn onto Trooper Lane itself and see a familiar sign indicating its unsuitability for heavy goods vehicles. The good news is that this lower portion of the climb is now tarmacked. The bad news is that the gradient increases to 26% towards residential terraced housing and you are reduced to the heaving, slow cadence marked by the steepest of climbs.

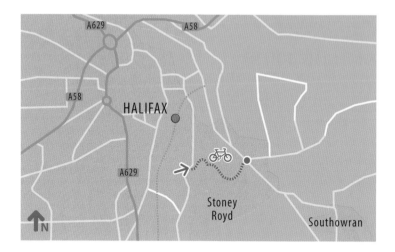

The road relents slightly for a short time through the estate, but only to between 11% and 15%.

The lane continues through a left-hand bend up the hillside where the real fun is about to begin. As the road steepens and pushes you towards your physical limit you are met with the sight of cobbles. As you hit the momentum-sapping stones, your bike may creak beneath you as the gradient exceeds 20% for a sustained period. The view down to Halifax and Calderdale is spectacular at this point, but your full attention will be on choosing the best line through the chaotic road surface. There is no respite except for a tiny 5-metre portion, yet beyond this the road gets steeper still and approaches 30%. You are now engaged in a personal war on this Calderdale hillside using every ounce of effort to reach the top of each pedal stroke.

The next left-hand bend takes you onto the final section of the climb. The gradient now dips below 20%, but the cobbles become older and have larger gaps, so you must maintain your concentration here as the summit approaches.

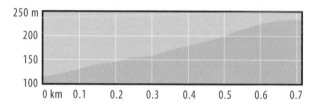

27. BUTTERTUBS PASS

FROM THE SOUTH

Difficulty	⦿⦿⦿⦿⦿⦿⦿⦿◯◯
Distance	3.8km
Av. Gradient	6.5%
Max. Gradient	23%
Height Gain	254m
Start Point	Simonstone Hall Hotel, Simonstone GR: 872915 (OS Landranger 98)
Local Cafés	The Cart House Tea Room, Hardraw, Hawes DL8 3LZ ☎ 01969 667691

Buttertubs Pass is a classic amongst classic Yorkshire climbs. It's frequently been a key element of elite road races, sportives and training routes. The exposure and dramatic scenery provide an experience that both cyclists and motorists appreciate. Indeed, motoring journalist Jeremy Clarkson described Buttertubs as 'England's only truly spectacular road'. Both sides of the pass are testing with extremely steep pitches followed by periods of relative calm. The route from

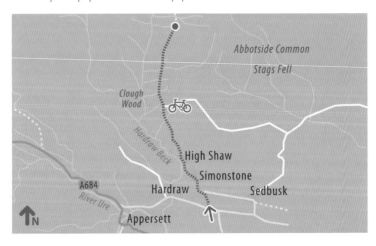

Muker in the North is the hardest, yet the southern ascent from Hawes cannot be ignored.

From the south, the serious climbing begins once through the hamlet of Simonstone and you hit a 9% slope above Hardraw Force waterfall on your left. After a bend right you are faced with four hard Buttertubs 'hits' in quick succession. The road inclines to 18% for 50 metres before levelling briefly, then rises again quickly to 16%. A 20-metre 'rest' then gives way to the third ramp, reaching 17%. By this point your legs are well and truly softened up, but the hardest part appears ahead. After another breather there's a brutal 100-metre spell, which touches 23% at its most extreme. It's unforgiving but the hardest section of the southern ascent is now over. There remains a prolonged stretch of classic Dales moorland tarmac where the gradient fluctuates around 3–6%, but includes short 10% 'kickers'. However, 20 hard pedal revs and these kickers are behind you, so you can concentrate on dodging rabbits or admire the view over to Great Shunner Fell on your way to the summit col.

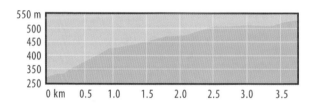

FROM THE NORTH

Difficulty	○○○○○○○○◐○
Distance	3.4km
Av. Gradient	6.8%
Max. Gradient	26%
Height Gain	256m
Start Point	Muker/Thwaite: turn north off B6270 signposted Hawes. GR: 893980 (OS Landranger 98)
Local Cafés	Muker Village Store and Tea Room, Muker, Richmond DL11 6QG ☎ 01748 886409

The tougher northern ascent begins just beyond Muker. There is an immediate steep ramp followed by a grind that hovers around 12% above the slopes of Cliff Beck. There is some easing for 200 metres and the road is slightly smoother before a further steep section arrives at 430 metres above sea level. This is the first of two very steep pitches switching back against the hillside of Great Shunner Fell. It's a steep start at 19%, which when combined with the frequent head wind makes this a serious ordeal. Following a short relent and switch-back, you are pitched again towards 20% as the road passes a viewpoint where sightseers may applaud your effort, if you are lucky.

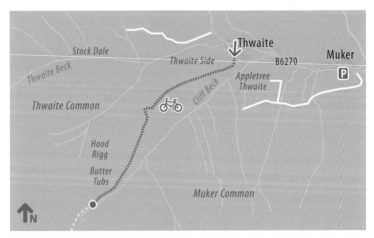

The gradient then becomes easier at 5% as you approach the beautifully engineered summit road.

With a precipitous hillside on your left, you crest the brow of a false summit to be met with the spectacular twisting and rolling road to the top. It's here you will pass the deep potholes known as the Buttertubs, so called because in years gone by, famers reputedly used them to cool butter on journeys from market on hot days. This road has a certain flawlessness and even the sight of the final daunting ramp ahead is exciting and punctuates the climb perfectly. It's about 200 metres of suffering on a slope reaching 26% with wind often being funnelled over the summit col. However, it doesn't last long and you are rewarded with an exhilarating decent and magnificent views to Wensleydale and beyond to Fleet Moss.

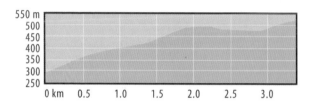

28. FLEET MOSS

Difficulty	⦿⦿⦿⦿⦿⦿⦿⦾○
Distance	2.6km
Av. Gradient	8.9%
Max. Gradient	22%
Height Gain	249m
Start Point	Gayle village exit. GR: 871891 (OS Landranger 98)
Local Cafés	Pennygarth Café, Market Place, Hawes DL8 3RD ☎ 08712 885608

Fleet Moss is one of those iconic climbs that all cyclists should ride at some point in their lifetime. It starts from Hawes with its quaint cafés and cobbled streets but as you turn off the main road past the primary school you can see the wild moors above. The signs to Kettlewell take you past the Wensleydale Creamery and once out of Gale village you begin to climb steeply for around 100 metres. This gives you the impression that the climb is now in full swing, but it's soon over and the gradient relents giving

way to a roll through the Sleddale valley with Dodd Fell towering above. The roads are narrow and the incline fluctuates gently over 1.5 kilometres until an abrupt ramp appears, over which there is a clear view of the remaining climb. The toughest part of the climb is now revealed and you can see the road clinging magnificently to the steep hillside. It's an exhilarating sight.

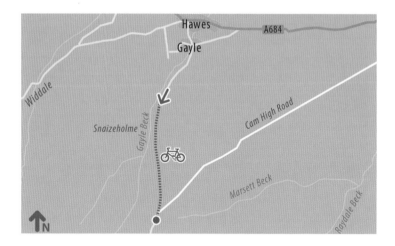

The road is grippy, but largely without potholes as the final three ramps approach. The first reaches 14%, forcing you out of the saddle; fencing shields you from the precipice on the right. A brief levelling takes you onto the penultimate stretch, first at 15% then to 22%. This is now brutal climbing and it's not unusual to be immersed in cloud by this point. The valleys of the Dales almost have their own weather systems where rain can cling on to one summit, whilst another can be bathed in sunshine, but this simply adds to the drama.

Fleet Moss saves the hardest slope until last as a brief 10% spell is followed by a ramp lasting 100 metres where you quickly reach 22% for a sustained period. This part pushes you hard but it quickly evens out over the top before another rolling segment towards the top of Fleet Moss itself. The descents on either slope are adrenaline-inducing, but the least technical is back to Hawes where it's possible to exceed 80kph (cross your fingers that no sheep cross your path!). A more sensible alternative might be to descend south and have a cake in Wharfedale. Either way, you should check your brakes.

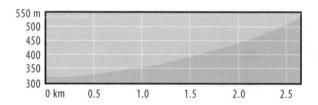

29. GUISE CLIFF

Difficulty	○○○○○○○○◐○
Distance	2.3km
Av. Gradient	9.2%
Max. Gradient	20%
Height Gain	208m
Start Point	Pateley Bridge/Bewerley: right bend and signpost to Bewerley Park and Otley. GR: 158646 (OS Landranger 99)
Local Cafés	The Old Granary Tea Shop, 17 High Street, Pateley Bridge HG3 5AP ☎ 08712 885608

Guise Cliff, also known as Nought Bank Road, is one of the best hill climbs and to reach it you must first climb south from Pateley Bridge then turn left on the minor road to Bewerley. The beginning is easy with a 400-metre stretch to spin the legs until you reach a signpost to Otley where the main climb begins towards an immaculate green hillside. The first section ascends at 8% for 100 metres on a fairly poor surface until you reach a left-hand bend when the slope pitches up twice, first to 20% then again to 16%.

The middle section is the hardest and begins where the road bends gradually right

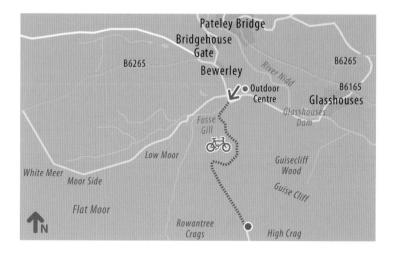

as you approach the treeline. As the road skirts the perimeter of woodland, the slope hits 14% then increases further to 20%. It's only a short pitch at this extreme gradient, but afterwards you will continue to strain on the pedals. The climb is especially hard now, forcing you into that 'physiological frontier' position, hung over the front axle for 200 metres or so. There is a further stinging 19% pitch until the slope becomes relatively gentle towards a delightful S-bend within a small nook amongst huge boulders. The road is steep as you pass through but you might just about remain in the saddle until you pass the path to Crocodile Rock where the gradient hits 16%.

You now ride on to the final section towards the moorland with a 100-metre section at 12%; York's Folly appears over to the left. The slope slowly relents but the prevailing head wind is horrendous and stunts your progress over these last few minutes. There are three more 150-metre sections of ever decreasing gradient until the road finally ceases its ascent. The first is 9% with the two successive sections dropping by 2% each time until the summit is reached with Guise Cliff itself now below you.

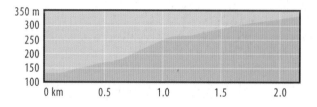

30. HARTWITH BANK

Difficulty	⦿⦿⦿⦿⦿⦿⦿⦿◯◯
Distance	1.6km
Av. Gradient	10.3%
Max. Gradient	24%
Height Gain	160m
Start Point	Summerbridge: turn off north from B6165 onto Harthwith Bank. GR: 202624 (OS Landranger 99)
Local Cafés	The Firs Tea Room, Summerbridge NG4 4JN ☎ 01423 781715

It's a tough task selecting the best climbs around Nidderdale but the climb of Hartwith Bank marginally trumps the rest due to its exceptionally steep first 500 metres and because it tops out at the fascinating Brimham Rocks.

A turn off the B6165 at Summerbridge takes you onto Hartwith Bank where the road carries you through a housing estate at 13%. It's a tough beginning to the climb, but it settles to 10% for most of the first 200 metres until you reach the perimeter of Old Spring Wood. Much of the road surface is coarse, although there are sections of smoother tarmac if you keep your eyes peeled. You will certainly have time to spot

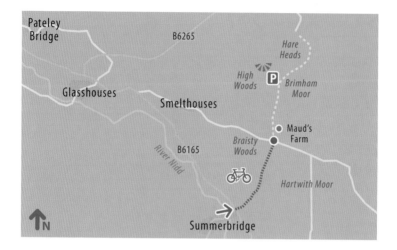

the smooth parts because your speed will reduce significantly as the slope becomes very steep for the next few minutes.

The initial 100 metres takes you to 17% around a right-hand curve in the road then a left-hand turn then takes you towards 20% on a sustained slope. The road is shrouded in dense woodland so it can be slippery at times. This means you might be forced to remain seated to aid traction, but doing so on this fierce incline is no mean feat. Up ahead there is literally some light at the end of the tunnel of trees, but the metaphor is misleading here as Hartwith Bank is not about to get easier. Indeed, the slope is about to become its most difficult.

As you pass some cottages on a right-hand bend the slope reaches 24% then continues beyond for 100 metres at 18% for a final ultra-demanding segment. If you can overcome this decisive incline you have effectively climbed Hartwith Bank. There is a 500-metre drag to the finish, which averages around 6%, but it is really no major obstacle. This brings you to a junction where Brimham Rocks can be seen.

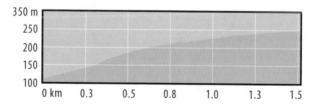

31. LANGBAR

Difficulty	⦿⦿⦿⦿⦿⦿⦿⦾⦾
Distance	1km
Av. Gradient	10.4%
Max. Gradient	20%
Height Gain	106m
Start Point	Beamsley: lane signposted Langbar heading east from Beamsley. GR: 078524 (OS Landranger 104)
Local Cafés	Abbey Tea Rooms, Ferry House, Bolton Abbey, Skipton BD23 6HB ☎ 01756 710797

The road passing Beamsley Beacon to Langbar is perhaps not at the top of the list of severe climbs, but it's a tough test that shouldn't be taken too lightly as it terminates with sustained pitch reaching 20%. The approach begins following a turning from the village of Beamsley, signposted 'Langbar'. Over the next 500 metres the road rolls pleasantly through gorse moorland over smooth roads with nothing over 9%. A right turn delivers the first view of the opening slope, which requires a significant increase in your concentration. This first pitch slowly but surely increases in steepness towards

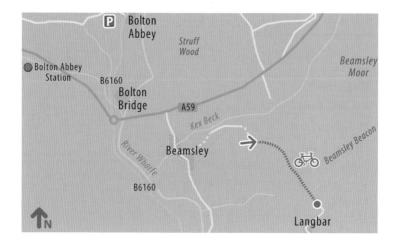

15%, as if riding from a concave bowl. The surface remains smooth, but the pedals subtly begin to turn more slowly and you begin to push harder and harder. This hors d'oeuvre is short-lived (100 metres), but is difficult enough to really sap your strength. Fortunately a short descent follows which allows you a breather for thirty seconds until the real fun begins.

The steepest section of the climb is clearly visible ahead and it is hard enough to force you straight from the saddle and the legs will begin to burn. It's a pretty spectacular view, but you'll need full commitment now as the road sustains a tough gradient eventually reaching 20%. It's a real lung-buster for 300 metres, taking you back into sustained oxygen debt and requiring a hefty dose of willpower to keep pushing.

Eventually the road levels to a comparatively easy 8% allowing a return to the saddle for 100 metres as you pass a small car park. The finish can now be seen and a short final ramp takes you to a house on the left marking an end to the climb, whilst the landscape towards Ilkley Moor opens up ahead.

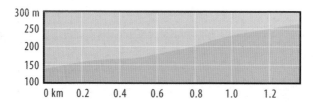

32. LANGCLIFFE SCAR

Difficulty	⬤⬤⬤⬤⬤⬤⬤⬤⬤◯
Distance	1.2km
Av. Gradient	11.9%
Max. Gradient	18%
Height Gain	140m
Start Point	Langcliffe: St John the Evangelist Church GR: 823650 (OS Landranger 98)
Local Cafés	Ye Olde Naked Man Café, Market Place, Settle BD24 9ED ☎ 01729 823230

Langcliffe Scar is a stretch of road that epitomizes the perfect British cycling climb. The ascent is gruelling and requires a high degree of fitness, whilst the surroundings are exceptional. The road is also reasonably quiet with a decent surface, allowing you to really commit yourself.

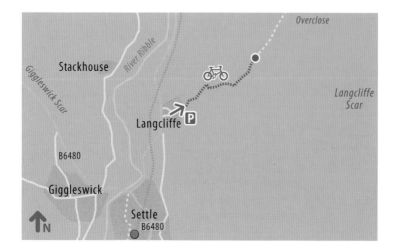

The village of Langcliffe in Ribblesdale marks the start point for the ascent. A relatively lenient opening leads all too quickly to a 17% pitch over 50 metres or so before you cross a cattle grid. This is merely a taste of what is to come and there is a short adjournment afterwards. So get your fill of the great view to the limestone outcrop of Stainforth Scar before the following section, the toughest of this climb.

A pleasing S-bend in the road is where the hardship begins. The tarmac is steep and damaged on the inside so attempt to take a wide path. However, you will be unable to escape this cruel ramp completely. You then head straight up at 18% for around 200 metres heaving the cranks with all your might. It's a remorseless stretch until you finally reach a sign warning of horses, where you can finally push a little less forcefully.

A left-hand bend marks the start of the last serious obstacle where the road steepens to 15% for a short period. As you crest the brow ahead, you will be able to see Yorkshire's three highest peaks of Ingleborough, Whernside and Pen-y-ghent. This is the stage for the infamous and incredibly punishing Three Peaks Cyclo-Cross race.

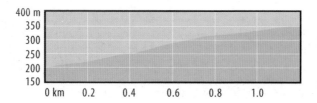

33. MALHAM

Difficulty	◎◎◎◎◎◎◎◎◯◯
Distance	2.1km
Av. Gradient	8.9%
Max. Gradient	20%
Height Gain	193m
Start Point	Malham: Town Head Farm/Campsite GR: 899632 (OS Landranger 98)
Local Cafés	The Olde Barn Café, The Old Barn, Malham BD23 4DA ☎ 01729 830486

There are a number of terrific climbs from the pretty village of Malham. The ascent of the Cove Road, passing to the west of Malham Cove, is the standout contender and has the advantage of a ringside view of one of the most spectacular natural wonders on these islands.

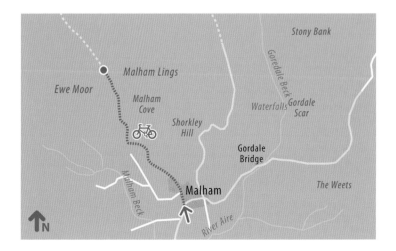

For the Cove Road take the first left after the Buck Inn pub in Malham. The first 400 metres are flat and pleasant, but at a left-hand bend the road inclines to 9% for 200 metres. A brief dip then leads to a short 15% ramp and another momentary let-up. Malham Cove can be seen over the wall on the right, dominating the view magnificently.

The road then turns and forces you to turn your back on the cove, perhaps because it requires your full attention. The road gets more grippy over 200 metres and the gradient reaches 19%. It's a typical out of the saddle grind until a slight recovery. This is followed by a right-hand bend back towards the cove – a 150-metre stretch which initially reaches 18%. The road reaches 20% here for an exhausting 50 metres, but thankfully the climb gets easier from now on, first to 12% then gradually to 7% over 300 metres. After a final flat roll, then a tight squeeze through a narrow section of road, you reach the summit. You are now high above Malham Cove and amongst the magnificent limestone pavements so typical of the Dales.

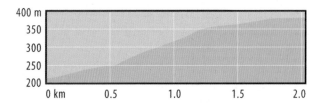

34. OXNOP SCAR

Difficulty	◉◉◉◉◉◉◉◉◉○
Distance	2.2km
Av. Gradient	11.3%
Max. Gradient	22%
Height Gain	246m
Start Point	Askrigg: Moor Road; turn left on off Main Street by Crown Inn Public House to Muker GR: 949912 (OS Landranger 98)
Local Cafés	Sykes Tea Room, Main Street, Askrigg ☎ 01969 650535

Oxnop Scar is an impressive crag perched high in the Yorkshire Dales on the ridge between Swaledale and Wensleydale. The more challenging southern approach features here.

As you turn off the main road through the village following the signpost to Muker you are quickly faced with the first steep pitch taking you beyond the 20% mark, and rapidly above the residential houses. It lasts for around 100 metres before levelling to around 5% for 400 metres. This is an opportunity for a good rest: you will be hit with several hard blows over the next few minutes.

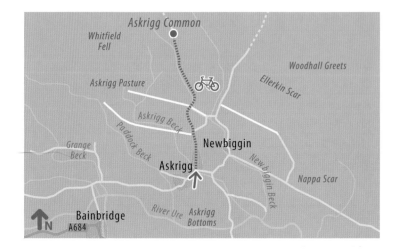

The second ramp begins after a junction where you must take the left-hand option to Muker. The slope exceeds 20% again, albeit briefly, before a breather for 100 metres or so, then a third section around 20%. The road is particularly smooth but by now the steep pitches will be taking their toll and your legs will be feeling heavy. You are then faced with a longer fourth stretch around 20%, which pushes you deeper into your reserves than before. Fortunately the incline relents for a short while so that you can steel yourself for the fifth and final really steep 100-metre ramp, which reaches 19%.

At this point you are close to the top and you will sense the slope easing. There is still work to do, however, as the climb becomes more of a drag compared to the stinging ramps so far. It's more sustained here, around 10–14% over a cattle grid and a false summit, before a final 13% sting taking you to the summit plateau. It's really worth continuing on to view Oxnop Scar if you have the energy. You could also attempt the northern ascent so that you can decide for yourself which is the best.

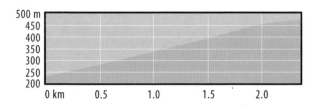

35. PARK RASH

Difficulty	◎◎◎◎◎◎◎◎◎◐
Distance	2.3km (from Kettlewell Beck)
Av. Gradient	10.2%
Max. Gradient	25%
Height Gain	231m
Start Point	Kettlewell: north-east exit of village on Cam Gill Road, signposted 'Leyburn' GR: 973725 (OS Landranger 98)
Local Cafés	The Cottage Tea Room, Kettlewell BD23 5QZ ☎ 01756 760405

Park Rash is one of those select number of super-steep climbs, hovering on the limit of what is possible when laying tarmac and riding a road bike. The climb begins in Kettlewell village as you turn left onto the lane signposted 'Leyburn', and you are immediately sent up a 1 in 4 slope. This initial shock is short-lived and you then experience a pleasant roll through trees above a secluded rural valley. You may even begin to wonder what all the fuss is about, but ahead you will catch a glimpse of what appears to be a road cutting across the hillside at an impossibly steep angle. You may even question whether it is indeed a road or a farmer's track, but you are not mistaken. This is Park Rash.

As you hit the slope you are reduced to an agonisingly sluggish churn. Any uncer-

tainty about your ability to ride up the slope will now be in sharp focus as you promptly select the easiest gear, whatever it is. What follows is several minutes of serious toil. The first 150 metres is unrelenting at 20% until you arrive at a left-hand bend where the road is scarred by the bottom of

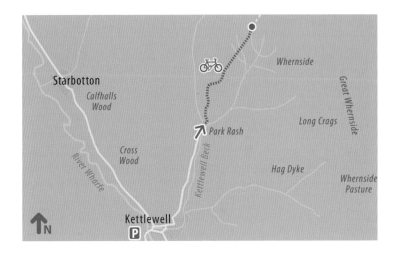

vehicles. The inside line is insanely steep, so take a wide approach if possible. The slope then hits 25% for a sustained period over 200 metres; there is little respite as you grind every pedal stroke and overcome the temptation to stop.

The gradient eventually eases and feels significantly easier of course, but the bumpy surface is unwelcome at this stage. The next few hundred metres consist of some classic roller-coaster Dales climbing where steep humps either entice you out of the saddle, or require thirty or so determined seated pedal revs to power over.

Finally up ahead and right you will spot the final part of the climb. It looks steep, but a short descent allows you to ready yourself for the final offensive. It is only 300 metres but the gradient rears up yet again to a muscle-burning 16–20% which, combined with the rough surface, just about finishes you off. A cattle grid marks the summit with the beautiful Coverdale road forming perfect territory for loosening off your aching legs. Alternatively, you could head back down and give your finger and arm muscles an equally strenuous workout.

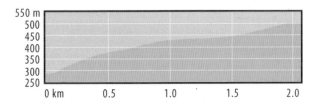

36. TRAPPING HILL

Difficulty	◉◉◉◉◉◉◉◉○○
Distance	1.7km
Av. Gradient	11.7%
Max. Gradient	20%
Height Gain	199m
Start Point	Lofthouse: turn right (north) from village signposted 'Masham'. GR: 102734 (OS Landranger 99)
Local Cafés	The Crown Hotel, Masham Road, Lofthouse, Harrogate HG3 5RZ ☎ 01423 755206

Trapping Hill is undoubtedly a very hard ascent, but it ranks amongst the most pleasing to ride. The road out of the village is signposted 'Masham' and you wind past the Crown Hotel and some quaint cottages. Once beyond these, the climb begins in earnest on a smooth surface at a steady 12% for 200 metres. The gradient eases slightly as the road sweeps right through delightful grassy meadows. However, it then steepens to a more demanding 17% incline over 250 metres with only a slight lull at half-way. This is the first of several really difficult sections, but you may find distraction in the magnificent view down Nidderdale to your right.

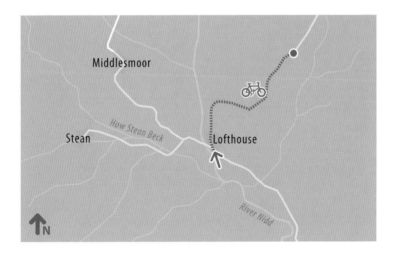

Fortunately there are short periods where the gradient relents and crucially there is now a 100-metre stretch at around 10% where you can have a short breather. The road remains smooth except for a few large metal grates on the left-hand gutter. Up ahead you will see the most demanding part of the climb as the road bends 90 degrees left and rears up to 18% over 100 metres. The road then turns sharp left again reaching 20% for a short, but potentially leg-breaking period. This can be a really cruel pitch especially if you have pushed too hard earlier on. The loose stones here provide an additional obstacle, but luckily the road quickly levels for 100 metres to a more forgiving 10% incline.

The final section is more sustained at around 14% for 200 metres so you can establish more of a tempo than before, although it's still a real strain to keep rolling. Eventually the gradient eases then slowly levels out on Lofthouse Moor. From here it's a steep descent back to Lofthouse, or you can follow the moorland road over to Masham.

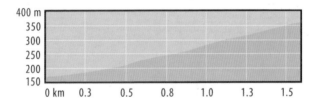

37. TURF MOOR

Difficulty	⬤⬤⬤⬤⬤⬤⬤◯◯
Distance	3.4km
Av. Gradient	5.5%
Max. Gradient	21%
Height Gain	240m
Start Point	Feetham: turn off B6270 north at the Punch Bowl Inn, signposted Langthwaite GR: 987985 (OS Landranger 98)
Local Cafés	Ghyllfoot Tea Room, Ghyllfoot, Gunnerside, Richmond DL11 6LA ☎ 01748 886239

Climbing north from Swaledale towards Arkengarthdale, Turf Moor is a hard but pleasing climb with a character that is different from many others described here. It's comprised of three distinct climbing sections separated by two short descents to moorland streams.

From the hamlet of Feetham, the road signposted to Langthwaite begins climbing steeply almost immediately. On a broken, gravelly surface through trees, the gradient exceeds 20% over a brutal 300-metre section. This really stings the legs but there is

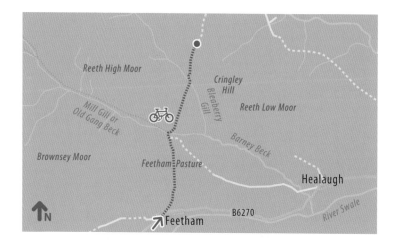

no doubt that this is the toughest part of the climb. The rest is not easy by any means but you won't be suspended over the handlebars for quite so long from now on.

The road levels a little on a left-hand bend, then more still over a cattle grid to around 10%. Open moorland views open to Swaledale to the right. A further steep section then levels to a steady plateau for 400 metres. It's a bumpy and exposed road until a view of the next part of the climb opens before you, winding up the hillside ahead. A short, steep decent here takes you to Barney Beck and a lovely stone bridge which then carries you on to the next uphill segment.

The climb from the beck is steep for around 100 metres, but soon the distinct rolling nature of these moorland roads returns; here you can begin to enjoy the exposure and wilderness around you. After a second steep and twisting descent you reach a cobbled ford across the stream. It is possible to ride through this, but take care here.

The third section of the Turf Moor climb takes you on a meandering, short but very steep pitch, the final tough gradient. The road soon becomes a more steady pull once more against a striking grey dry stone wall towards the summit.

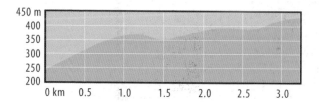

38. ACKLAM BROW

Difficulty	⊘⊘⊘⊘⊘⊘⊘○○○
Distance	1km
Av. Gradient	9.4%
Max. Gradient	20%
Height Gain	93m
Start Point	Acklam: Eastern exit of village at junction with lane signposted to Barthorpe GR: 785617 (OS Landranger 100)
Local Cafés	Pattacakes, Main Street, Welburn YO60 7DX ☎ 01759 377392

The question of which Wolds climb is toughest is debatable, but Acklam Brow would certainly form part of such a discussion. This is a seriously hard climb heading north

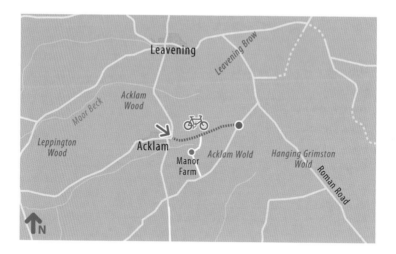

from the sleepy village of Acklam. It may be relatively short, but it should not be underestimated.

As you exit the village on a steep section, you will see a right turn to Birdsall, which you must follow. The road flattens for 100 metres until a sign indicates the really serious 20% slopes ahead, and almost immediately the narrow road ramps up. First it is 10% but gradually you are forced into the easiest gear and are tempted out of the saddle. Visually the road doesn't appear that steep, but the sensations from the pedals are your most accurate barometer. It is steep for sure.

Amongst deep hedges the gradient reaches 20% as you pass a farmhouse. Such steep inclines are not always so alarming unless they are relatively sustained, but on this occasion the gradient continues for long enough to cause serious discomfort. There is a brief levelling, but the road steepens again towards 20% and you will be drooped over the bars. The road surface is good here and the gradient eventually levels to 8% as you reach the TV mast that once stood so far above.

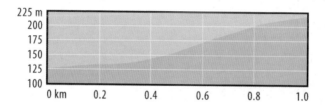

39. BLACK BROW

Difficulty	◯◯◯◯◯◯◯◯◯◯
Distance	2.2km
Av. Gradient	10.4%
Max. Gradient	25%
Height Gain	235m
Start Point	Grosmont train station GR: 828053 (OS Landranger 94)
Local Cafés	Old School Coffee Shop, Grosmont, Whitby YO22 5QW ☎ 01947 895754

As you cross the railway lines taking the road east out of Grosmont you begin climbing very steeply for 200 metres. The gradient reaches 16% until a right turn to Goathland and Pickering where a sign warns of an impending 33% slope. It is certainly a brutal ramp to 20% for 50 metres but the road is as smooth as silk before a short section of respite. The road ramps again to 22% for 50 metres then levels again to 15% where you meet a right-hand bend.

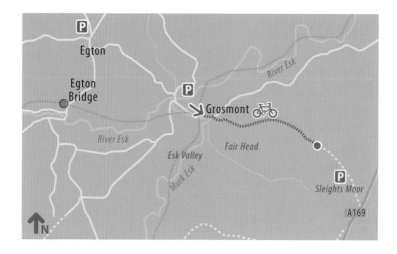

You are about to hit the hardest section of the climb. The 33% warning passed earlier is reinforced here by a second sign and you can see the road rising up ahead, straight and sustained. The true gradient reaches 25%, not as steep as the signs suggest, but this slight exaggeration does not detract from the severity of this climb.

The hardest part of the climb is behind you once over this steep pitch but there remains a kilometre or so of hard work. First there is a short period of rolling road between 5% and 10% where the views open, followed by a long sustained drag at 10% where you can settle into a steady but hard rhythm. After this it gets a little easier at around 7% when Whitby appears on the distant horizon to the east. It's a nice climb where you can enjoy the view until the gradient reaches 9% again over a final pull to the summit. By now it's easy to forget the super-hard beginning to this climb, but a look behind at the height gained will remind you that you have just scaled one of the toughest climbs in Yorkshire.

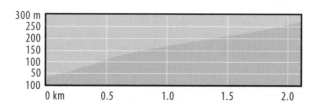

40. BLAKEY BANK

Difficulty	⊙⊙⊙⊙⊙⊙⊙⊙◯
Distance	1.2km
Av. Gradient	13%
Max. Gradient	20%
Height Gain	172m
Start Point	Church Houses: Long Lane, junction with Short Lane, track to Head House Farm GR: 674978 (OS Landranger 94)
Local Cafés	Dale Head Farm Tea Room, Rosedale East, Pickering YO18 8RL ☎ 01751 417353

Rising from the agricultural valley of Farndale, Blakey Bank is both feared and respected by local riders. To experience the full climb you should start from the hamlet of Church Houses from where an easy tootle along a narrow lane leads to an increasingly steep opening slope. From here you can see the road winding its way up to the imposing Blakey Ridge.

As you pass a road junction the gradient has already reached 15%, but the most intense climbing is about to commence. It is fairly obvious which road to take at the

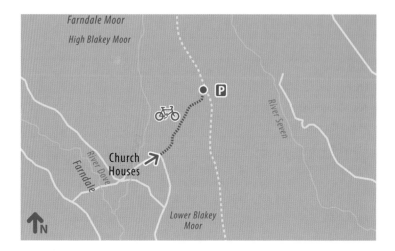

junction: the road straight ahead goes skyward. Over a sustained 150-metre stretch the gradient reaches 17% then levels significantly for a while. Recover here and brace yourself for the rest of the journey, as it is pretty relentless from now on.

The spectacular view across High Blakey Moor appears as you hit a short ramp, which requires a few hard pushes on the pedals to overcome. The slope then becomes harder and harder as you pass a car park on the left. You will now see the road becoming frighteningly steep up ahead, marking the hardest part of the climb. The gradient touches 20% until a momentary breather, then rears up to 20% again for 50 metres. There are numerous grit bins that can be used for markers as this super-hard section pushes you further into the red. Unfortunately you will remain in the red and struggle to clear the lactic acid for the remaining 200 metres of the climb, which fluctuates between 13% and 16%. A final short steep ramp takes you to the summit and Blakey Ridge Road where you can more knowledgeably assess where it rates amongst the toughest climbs.

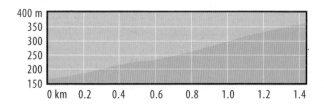

41. CARLTON BANK

Difficulty	⊙⊙⊙⊙⊙⊙⊙⊙○○
Distance	1.9km
Av. Gradient	10.1%
Max. Gradient	22%
Height Gain	190m
Start Point	Carlton in Cleveland: village exit road south on Alum House Lane signposted Chop Gate GR: 510042 (OS Landranger 93)
Local Cafés	Roots Farm Shop, Home Farm, East Rounton DLE 2LE ☎ 01609 882480

The climb starts as you leave the village of Carlton in Cleveland where the Cleveland Hills tower menacingly above. Thankfully this early phase is fairly kind for 500 metres until reaching Busby Wood. It then ramps steadily towards 13% on a gentle left-hand bend. It's a pleasant ride through the trees, but the road becomes increasingly steep, reaching 15% and slowing progress. Carlton Bank is now beginning to tighten its grip and squeezes further towards 22% before easing briefly. You then ride over a cattle grid making the transition to the heather moorlands and the foot of the steepest part

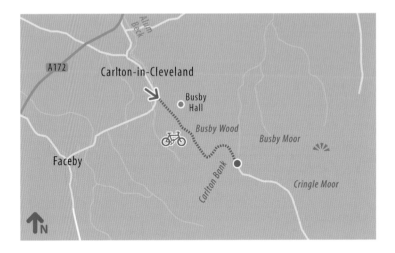

of the bank. The gradient is 19% as you approach, but suddenly the road bends 90 degrees to the left to cut across the hillside so it remains within sensible parameters of steepness.

The next section is where Carlton Bank becomes a cruel master hitting you with recurring hurtful ramps, whilst teasing you with false visions of the summit. The first slope reaches 21% over 50 metres then levels to 7% before bending gradually right and steepening again to 21%. The road is rough as you cross a stone wall supporting the road on the steep hillside. The view over the precipice to the left is glorious. The dramatically steep bank with scree slopes is highlighted against a patchwork of valley fields comprising a myriad of yellow and green shades.

After a short breather, the road steepens again to 20%. The summit feels close now but you will be tempted to reserve your judgment as you will have been fooled before now. Yet the summit does come after a grind, then a final 17% flourish until the road flattens rapidly amongst the sightseer's cars parked on Cringle Moor.

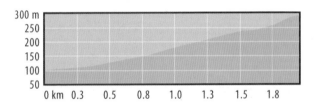

42. EGTON MOOR

Difficulty	⊘⊘⊘⊘⊘⊘⊘⊘○○
Distance	2.3km
Av. Gradient	9.1%
Max. Gradient	23%
Height Gain	210m
Start Point	Egton Bridge: Horseshoe Hotel; Lane junction signposted to Rosedale GR: 802052 (OS Landranger 94)
Local Cafés	Hazelwood Tea Rooms, Front Street, Grosmont, Whitby YO22 5QE ☎ 01947 895292

The path to follow from Egton Bridge is signposted 'Rosedale' and offers an easy beginning amongst thick hedgerows. There is a customary, but exaggerated, 33% gradient sign as the road becomes steeper and forces you upright. This is the beginning of the first of three distinct sections of the climb. This initial 600 metres is characterized by a number of short but very arduous pitches, with two small 15% ramps to begin with. These are separated by sections of recovery as you rise amongst the meadows

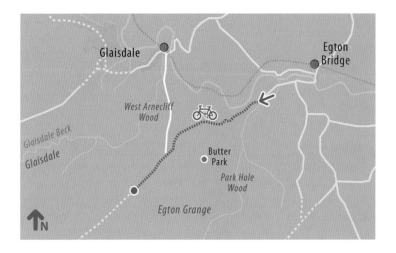

towards hillside farms and cottages. As you reach one of these, the gradient becomes more severe, reaching 18%, but as you ride through an S-bend, that increases to 23%. It is an intense minute or so, and by the end of this cruel 200 metres you will be nicely cooked. Thankfully there is a chance to rest as you pass the last few houses.

The second section of the climb begins here and features less brutal slopes, but a more prolonged rollercoaster mixture of easy periods interspersed with strenuous rises. This transition stage continues for 1,500 metres while still within the view-blocking, but sheltering confines of dense hedges. The road is straight and you can see the undulating terrain stretching before you, continuously climbing between 6% and 13%.

The final section of the climb begins as you pass a cattle grid and enter a noticeably different moorland stage, including a long straight road amongst deep heather where you can sit in the saddle and drive the pedals in a more metronomic style. The gradient remains around 3% taking you gradually to 300 metres above sea level and an isolated, windswept plateau.

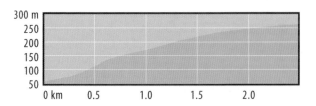

43. GLAISDALE HEAD

Difficulty	⊙⊙⊙⊙⊙⊙⊙⊙⊙⊙
Distance	1.3km
Av. Gradient	14.2%
Max. Gradient	22%
Height Gain	180m
Start Point	Glaisdale Valley Head; at junction of lanes take right fork signposted Rosedale GR: 743030 (OS Landranger 94)
Local Cafés	Woolly Sheep Café, North York Moors Centre, Lodge Lane YO21 2NB ☎ 01439 772737

Glaisdale Head, or Caper Hill, is one of the top three hardest ascents in the Peak District and Yorkshire. The road surface is rough and unforgiving, the wind is often against you, and the slope is incessantly steep for just about the whole journey.

The serious climbing begins after a right turn towards Rosedale following a steady 3-kilometre pull up the valley from Glaisdale village. The narrow, rarely driven lane weaves for a short distance until the first very steep 20% pitch appears. The lane is so isolated from traffic that the centre is highlighted with green vegetation, which appears almost luminescent in the daylight. The non-vegetated peripheries form your path but they are rough, costing you energy that you desperately need.

The next 50 metres is the easiest section of the whole climb, but is still 15%. It

is likely you will already be out of the saddle here and, unless you have mountain bike gearing, you will spend much of the next few minutes in this position as you try to lever the pedals forward. Yet it gets steeper ahead amongst the bracken, thick hedges and oak trees.

The ascent is notable for straight and steep ramps punctuated by very short level ter-

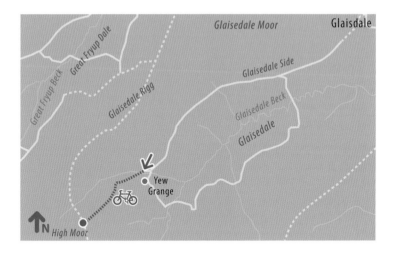

races, which offer a momentary opportunity to push a little less hard for a few pedal revolutions. The next 100 metres takes you to 22% as you reach the halfway point. The gradient is punishing enough but ahead lies the most hideously placed cattle grid in the whole of Yorkshire. Just when you reach the limits of physical endurance you need to push even harder to make it safely over the obstacle.

The cattle grid marks the transition to open moorland where a head wind can become a factor. The gradient remains around 17% for a short time then returns to 20% as the road straightens. There's another 3m levelling then the steep drag just keeps going until you reach a gravelled parking spot on the left. Here you may just be able to remain seated for a while on this 14% slope, but again it gets steeper for 200 metres. There's no escape and you're likely to be chewing your handlebar tape by now. Finally, the road does begin to relent significantly over the last 100 metres but it's too little, too late. This really is one of the most brutal, unforgiving climbs to be found anywhere.

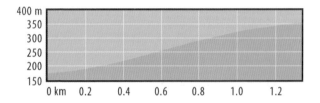

44. HEYGATE BANK

Difficulty	⊙⊙⊙⊙⊙⊙⊙⊙◐○
Distance	1.6km
Av. Gradient	9.8%
Max. Gradient	23%
Height Gain	154m
Start Point	Rosedale Abbey: lane north-east signposted Egton GR: 724959 (OS Landranger 94)
Local Cafés	Abbey Tea Room, Rosedale Abbey, Pickering YO18 8SA ☎ 01751 417475

If you travel to Rosedale for the first time with a bike, it's likely you will be there with a view to having a crack at Rosedale Chimney, and rightly so. However, the ascent of Heygate Bank, on the opposite side of the valley, is only slightly easier and leads you to some of the other classic climbs described in this book.

The beginning, past houses on the edge of Rosedale village, is fairly sedate except for a short 12% ramp, though the surface on this early phase is badly broken and you

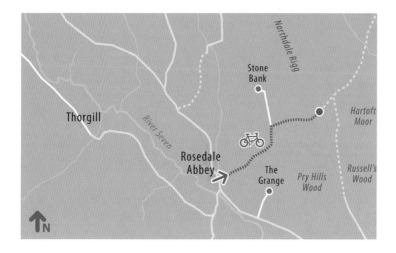

have to concentrate on choosing the smoothest route. The undulating road passes under the shelter of trees and then becomes more and more severe. A ramp takes you to 17% then yields, but quickly returns to 15% before relenting once again. Up ahead it rises further as you ride towards a left-hand bend.

Approaching the bend, the slope reaches 21% and it's clear that the gradient is not going to relent. It reaches 23% after the bend and there is almost no let-up for 150 metres. This section is cruel and makes the pistons squeal. A slight reprieve comes when the road bends right but, as is commonplace on Yorkshire moors, a cattle grid appears while still climbing at 15%. After this hurdle, the road becomes a sticky drag for a short while, but then begins to steepen yet again towards an apparent summit crest. Spirits lift as you realize the end is near, but the gradient touches 19% on this increasingly steep finish. You may be tempted to fire the afterburners but the climb is not finished just yet. A further 100 metres continues at 11% to the Rosedale Moor where you can continue your ride over to Egton or Glaisdale.

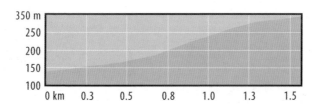

45. MURTON BANK

Difficulty	◐◐◐◐◐◐◐◐○○
Distance	1.1km
Av. Gradient	11.2%
Max. Gradient	25%
Height Gain	126m
Start Point	Hawnby: bridge over River Rye GR: 543893 (OS Landranger 100)
Local Cafés	Hawnby Stores and Tea Room, Front Street, Hawnby YO62 5QR ☎ 01439 798223

The climb up Murton Bank heads south from Hawnby and forms a trio of challenging climbs which could be linked together during one ride (the other two are Nos 48 and 50).

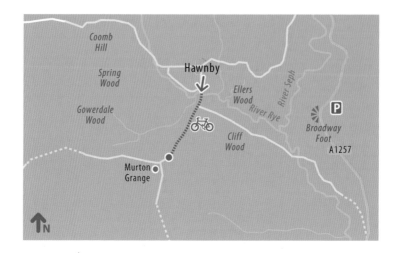

As you cross the River Rye the climb begins quickly heading towards the domed, tree-covered hillside above. This first pitch reaches 17% on a narrow lane enclosed by 3-metre-high hedges until the road levels a little past a junction. Here you must continue straight on towards Boltby and onto the steepening slope ahead, which reaches 14% initially, then 25% as you head into Cliff Wood. This really makes you heave, weave and blow, but there is a short, slightly easier section soon afterwards, so you can recover slightly. However, the pain isn't over quite yet as the road inclines again to 18% for a fairly sustained period pushing you back into the red zone.

After the severity of these opening 600 metres there is a significantly easier period where the gradient is first 12% becoming progressively more comfortable at 5%. There is then a final pinch at 17% over 50 metres but you might be able to power over this if you have saved some energy previously. You now have the really steep slope behind you so can drive over the final drag as you surface from the tree line and the views appear.

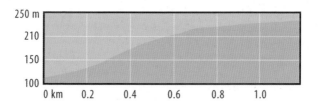

46. ROBIN HOOD'S BAY

Difficulty	⊙⊙⊙⊙⊙⊙⊙⊙○○
Distance	3km
Av. Gradient	7%
Max. Gradient	25%
Height Gain	219m
Start Point	Robin Hood's Bay: coastguard visitor centre, sea front. GR: 954049 (OS Landranger 94)
Local Cafés	Swell Café, The Old Chapel, Chapel Street, Robin Hood's Bay, Whitby YO22 4SQ ☎ 01947 880180

Robin Hood's Bay is a quaint fishing community and it's here in the heart of the oldest part of the village that the climb begins. The road is easy until the Laurel Inn. The lane then ramps up dramatically to 25% over 100 metres taking you rapidly from the old town back to the main road. It's a steep pitch, but there is now time to recover as you take Thorpe Lane left to Scarborough and wind your way over 1 kilometre through the adjoining town of Fylingthorpe.

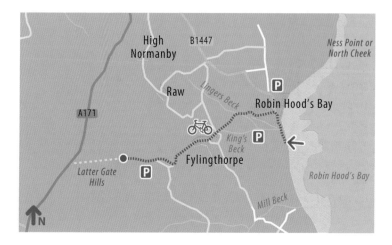

As you exit Fylingthorpe the serious climbing begins again at around 10% beyond the final houses. Then as you reach a left-hand bend it gets more painful with a 17% pitch. The climb doesn't relent enough to give you a decent recovery from here on, so prepare yourself for a few minutes of suffering as you follow the road up the hillside sign-posted 'Scarborough'. The gradient remains around 13%, but thankfully you will be well sheltered from the prevailing wind. However, the road gradually begins to emerge from the hedgerows and the wind does become a major factor and a tougher incline is yet to come.

If you have a GPS it will initially register 19% as you reach the beginning of the end, but it then relents a little over a straight but turgid 200 metres. Up ahead you can see the top, yet it's still some way off. However, it's apparent that there is a final sting in this climb. The sting is only short and, when you conquer this final 20% gradient, the climb to Fylingdales Moor is complete. Now the whole of Yorkshire lies in front of you but make sure to look back at this point, as the view over the bay is magnificent.

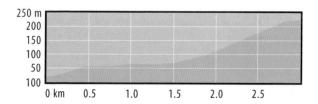

47. ROSEDALE CHIMNEY

Difficulty	⦿⦿⦿⦿⦿⦿⦿⦿⦿◯
Distance	1.4km
Av. Gradient	12.6%
Max. Gradient	30%
Height Gain	183m
Start Point	Rosedale Abbey; lane south at Blue Rosedale Chimney Bank signpost GR: 725957 (OS Landranger 94)
Local Cafés	Graze on the Green Tea Room, 12 Rosedale Abbey, Pickering YO18 8SA ☎ 01751 417468

Rosedale Chimney, known as the 'Chain Breaker', is amongst the hardest of cycling climbs in the country. It begins from Rosedale in the heart of the North York Moors and the route south to Rosedale Bank is clearly marked with a striking blue warning sign reading, 'Rosedale Chimney Bank, ½ mile ahead, Gradient 1 in 3'.

You travel over a bridge then begin climbing at 9% with little to indicate the ordeal lying ahead. At this stage there is the unavoidable view of the gigantic hillside to your right, dominating your peripheral vision. You might attempt to ignore it but you are fully aware of the extraordinary scale of the landscape around you. It's probably best not to look upwards.

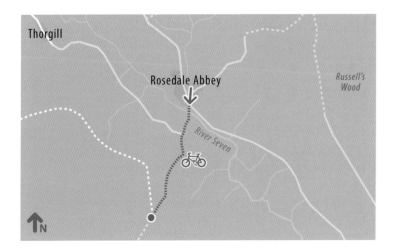

As you pass the White Horse pub you are forced from the saddle on a relatively easy 13% gradient then a right-hand bend where you reach 19%. Here, you'll notice how high above the valley you have already climbed as you head towards the cattle grid marking the start of the merciless middle section. As you ride beyond the treeline and into the open moorland, the climb gets really difficult for the next few minutes. The switchback that marks the halfway point takes you beyond 20% and there is the realization that you are on an abnormally severe climb. But it's about to get steeper. The road ramps up ahead towards 30% over a short but brutal section where every sinew screams in pain.

The road begins to level and you justifiably revel in the triumph of cresting the steepest sections of the climb. But though the worst is over there's still work to do. The 15% gradient relents to 9% and you become increasingly aware of the spectacular views to your left. There is a short 15% 'kicker' but you have now succeeded in ascending one of the most iconic climbs in the entire country.

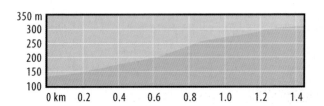

48. SNECK YATE BANK

Difficulty	⊙⊙⊙⊙⊙⊙⊙⊙⊙
Distance	0.9km
Av. Gradient	14.9%
Max. Gradient	26%
Height Gain	141m
Start Point	Boltby: bridge over Lunshaw Beck GR: 498869 (OS Landranger 100)
Local Cafés	Sutton Bank Tea Rooms, Sutton Bank, Thirsk YO7 2EX ☎ 01845 597962

The climb starts from the small village of Boltby and a fairly strenuous pull in itself, but the following gentle roll through the serene valley is a joy. The first few hundred metres are rolling with pitches at 9–15% which are hard, but do not compare to what is to come. The road steepens further past Heskwith Grange before a brief levelling for 20 metres. The view of the coniferous woodland that opens following a right-hand bend is the signal to prepare yourself for the crux. The peacefulness of the cows

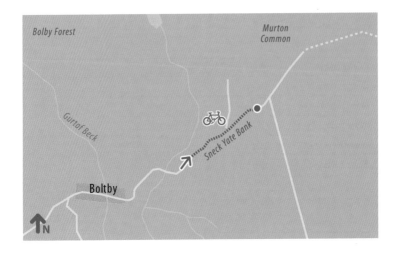

grazing in the alpine-like meadows above is in direct contrast to the concern that you may be experiencing as you see the road steepening ahead.

As you pass High Paradise Farm the gradient exceeds 16% and skid marks on the tarmac suggest that this is getting excessive now, yet it gets steeper still. You will be hung over the handlebars, heaving, rocking and rolling on the bike, straining to maintain your momentum. This really is a hideous section that steepens further to 26% and stays super-hard for 100 metres. You become acutely aware of your slow speed and throbbing heart within a bubble of concentration and suffering. This part of the climb is relentless.

An S-bend brings a section at 16–18% which, in the crazy world of tough hill climbing, is significantly more straightforward than what has gone before. It lasts for 60 metres – long enough, but you sense that the summit is around the corner. And so it is, with a small push you reach a more gradual slope taking you towards a car park used by mountain bikers keen to experience Boltby Forest.

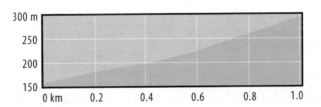

49. STREET HILL

Difficulty	⊚⊚⊚⊚⊚⊚⊚⊚⊚○
Distance	1.6km
Av. Gradient	9.9%
Max. Gradient	21% (optional 30% for 10 metres at junction)
Height Gain	165m
Start Point	Bridge over Great Fryup Beck GR: 730046 (OS Landranger 94)
Local Cafés	Woolly Sheep Café, North York Moors Centre, Lodge Lane, Danby YO21 2NB ☎ 01439 772737

Street Hill has received far less attention than some household names such as Rosedale Chimney and Sneck Yate Bank, yet this classic climb is equal to anything in the county and deserves respect. The main ascent is reached via a grippy climb through Great Fryup Dale followed by a short descent to Great Fryup Beck where the road can be seen zig-zagging its way up the hillside. On crossing a bridge over the beck the gradient increases, gently at first, then touches 8% before reaching the small hamlet of Street. This is the point where the climb becomes harsh and will continue in unrelenting fashion until Glaisdale Rigg is reached much higher above.

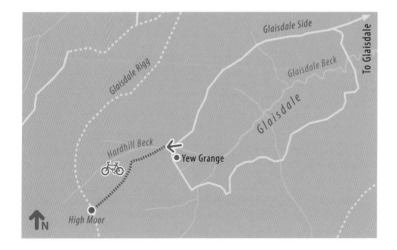

The road leading out of Street is arrow straight and gradually ramps up over 200 metres until the incline touches 20%. The climb then follows the road to Rosedale at a junction where, over a few metres, it gets steeper still at around 30% if you dare take the direct path. This vicious step takes you on to a narrower and rougher lane where the gradient remains around 19% until easing a little. This is the easiest section of the climb and offers the best opportunity to admire the magnificent view over Fryup Dale. However this 'easy' section is short-lived and becomes leg-screamingly steep yet again towards a zig-zag back across the hillside.

It's likely you will have spent a significant amount of time out of the saddle by now and you will remain so over the next 100 metres where there is a pitch touching 21%. After this it gets only slightly easier as you reach a cattle grid taking you on to the open Glaisdale moorland. Finally the slope becomes more manageable around 10% through the heather until a right-hand bend propels you upward again to 18% over 100 metres over the top to the summit and Glaisdale Rigg.

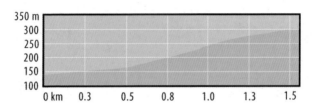

50. WHITE HORSE BANK

Difficulty	⦾⦾⦾⦾⦾⦾⦾⦾⦾◯
Distance	1.5km
Av. Gradient	11.5%
Max. Gradient	20%
Height Gain	172m
Start Point	Kilburn: turn off Carr Lane left and north (signposted 'White Horse'). GR: 514805 (OS Landranger 100)
Local Cafés	Coxwold Tea Rooms, The School House, Coxwold, York YO61 4AD ☎ 01347 868077

On leaving the quiet village of Kilburn you'll see the striking shape of a white horse clinging to the steep, tree-covered hillside high above. A left-hand turn is signposted 'White Horse Bank' and you soon hit the first of several short but incredibly steep ramps. As you enter the woodland the gradient hovers around 20% for a brutal 100 metres until a momentary lull. After a few pedal strokes you hit another steep 20% pitch on a right-hand bend where there are the customary vehicle scrapes on the inside of the bend. Another short breather follows but yet again you are pitched towards 17%.

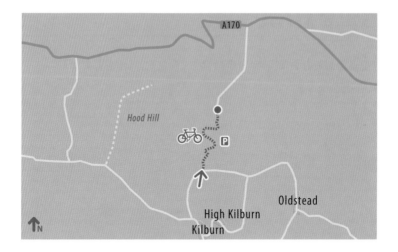

There is another brief let-up but over the next 200 metres the gradient progressively reaches 15% leading to a tourist car park. It's surprising, but satisfying to see you are now just underneath the White Horse itself that seemed so far above just a few minutes ago. Yet considering the rate of climb so far you might even expect to be at the top by now, but the hillside in front indicates you have much more work yet to do. You may well be fairly worn out, but you need to persevere: there are only a few more minutes to go.

The final stage offers tantalizing views through the trees to the right. It's the easiest section since the foot of the climb where, except for a short 17% ramp, there is a 200 metres stretch around 9% until a left-hand bend. The final severe pitch is next and you are taken to 19% through an S-bend as the sky gradually emerges around eye level. You might feel sure that the summit is around this corner and go kamikaze through the steepest, most direct line, but there is still a little more. Indeed, a final push takes you to a rapidly flattening road where you can now easily spin the legs.

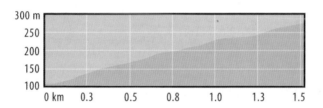

BIKE SHOPS

PEAK DISTRICT & SOUTH YORKSHIRE

Peak Cycle Sport
Wood Street Mill, Pickford Street,
Macclesfield, SK11 6JQ
01625 426333
peakcyclesport.com

Buzz Cycles
12 Bridge Street, Belper, DE56 1AX
01773 307325
buzzcycles.co.uk

Parsley Hay Cycle Hire
Parsley Hay, Biggin, SK17 0DG
01298 84493
parsleyhay.co.uk

Zepnat Cycles
127 Smedley Street, Matlock, DE4 3JG
01629 593631
zepnat.com

Stanley Fearn Cycles
19 Bakewell Road, Matlock, DE4 3AU
01629 582089
stanleyfearns.co.uk

18 Bikes
8 Castleton Rd, Hope, S33 6RD
01433 621111; 07734 653006
18bikes.co.uk

Bike Garage
High Peak Garden Centre, Hope Road,
Bamford, S33 0AL
01433 659345
bikegarage.co.uk

Pelican Cycles
1 Old Road, Brampton, Chesterfield, S40
2RE
01246 767078
pelicancycles.co.uk

Langsett Cycles
182–192 Infirmary Rd, Sheffield, S6 3DH
0114 2348191
langsettcycles.co.uk

J E James Cycles
347–361 Bramall Lane, Sheffield, S2 4RN
0114 2550557
jejamescycles.co.uk

Tony Butterworth Cycles
86–90 Catch Bar Lane, Sheffield, S6 1TA
0114 2343218
tonybutterworths.com

Evans Cycles
164–170 Queens Rd, Sheffield, S2 4DH
0114 2172700
evanscycles.com

Wilson Cycles
220 City Road, Sheffield, S2 5HP
0114 2723483
wilsoncycles.co.uk/shop/index.php

Decathlon
199 Eyre St, Sheffield, S1 3HU
0114 2298190
decathlon.co.uk

The Bike Tree
289a Abbeydale Road South, Sheffield, S17
3LB
0114 2365858
thebiketree.co.uk

Edinburgh Bicycle Co-Operative
300 Broadfield Road, Sheffield, S8 0XQ
0114 2558580
edinburghbicycle.com

Race Scene
210 Sheffield Rd, Barnsley, S70 5TF
01226 291888
racescene.co.uk

Planet X
6 Ignite, Magna Way, S60 1FD
01709 386666
planet-x-bikes.co.uk

The Bike Factory
Vernon House, Beech Road, Whaley Bridge,
SK23 7HP
01663 735020
ukbikefactory.com

Sett Valley Cycles
9 Union Road, New Mills, SK22 3EL
01663 742629
settvalleycycles.co.uk

High Peak Cycles
2 Smithy Fold, Glossop, SK13 8DD
01457 861535
highpeakcycles.co.uk

Freeride Cycles
20 Market Street, Disley, SK12 2AA
01663 764444
freeridecycles.com

WEST YORKSHIRE

Try Cycling
9a North Rd, Kirkburton, HD8 0NX
01484 607830
trycycling.co.uk

Just Ride
21 Fleet St, Scissett, HD8 9JJ
07814 343291

Wheelspin Cycles
Victoria Mills, Albert St, Huddersfield, HD1
3PR
01484 533338
wheelspincycles.com

Velocity Cycles
70 Acre Street, Lindley, HD3 3EL
01484 455300
velocitycycles-huddersfield.co.uk

V S Cycles
19 Bradford Road, Brighouse, HD6 1RW
01484 500860
vscycles.co.uk

Cyclegear
68 Horton St, Halifax, HX1 1QE
01422 344602
ukbikesdepot.com

Shay Cycles
46 South Parade, Halifax, HX1 2LY
01422 367244
shaycycles.co.uk

Blazing Saddles
35 West End, Hebden Bridge, HX7 8UQ
01422 844435
blazingsaddles.co.uk

Pedal Sport Ltd
193–195 King Cross Rd, Halifax, HX1 3LN
01422 361460
pedalsport.co.uk

All Terrain Cycles
Salts Mill, Victoria Rd, Saltaire, BD18 3LA
01274 588488
allterraincycles.co.uk

Pennine Cycles
1019 Thornton Rd, Bradford, BD8 0PA
01274 881030
penninecycles.com

Paul Milnes Cycles
Unit 4H Hillam Court, Hillam Rd, Bradford,
BD2 1QN
01274 308860
paulmilnescycles.com

BIKE SHOPS

Keith Lambert Cyclesports
108 Main Street, Bingley, BD16 2JH
01274 560605
keithlambertcycles.co.uk

Ellis Briggs Cycles
Otley Rd, Shipley, BD17 7DS
01274 583221
ellisbriggscycles.co.uk

Aire Valley Cycles
Millennium House 74, South Street, Shipley,
BD21 1DQ
01535 288709
airevalleycycles.com

Firth Cycles
72 West End, Queeensbury, BD13 2ER
01274 817483
firthcycles.com

Crosstrax
1 The Crescent, Leeds, LS16 6AA
0113 2610120
crosstrax.co.uk

Jedi Cycle Sport
Lingdale Baxter Wood, Crosshills, Keighley,
BD20 8BB
01535 810045
jedicyclesport.co.uk

J D Cycles
42a Nelson Rd, Ilkley, LS29 8HN
01943 816101
jdcycles.co.uk

Chevin Cycles
Gay Lane, Otley, LS21 1BR
01943 462773
chevincycles.com

Dirt Wheels
66 Boroughgate, Otley, LS21 1AE
01943 466869
dirtwheels.co.uk

YORKSHIRE DALES AND NIDDERDALE

Stif Cycles
The Beech New York Mills, Summerbridge,
HG3 4LA
01423 780738
stif.co.uk

Dave Ferguson Cycles
3 Albion Yard, Skipton, BD23 1ED
01756 795367
davefergusoncycles.com

Riders Cycle Centre
Unit 3 Engine Shed Lane, Skipton, BD23 1UP
07826 721463
riderscyclecentre.com

3 Peaks Cycles
Market Place, Settle, BD24 9EJ
01729 824232
3peakscycles.com

Escape Bike Shop
Kirksteads Westhouse, Ingleton, LA6 3NJ
015242 41226
escapebikeshop.com

Boneshakers
Unit 13, Regent House, 11 Albert St,
Harrogate, HG1 1JX
01423 259721
boneshakersbikes.co.uk

Cycopath Cycles
1 Laver View, Ripon, HG4 3NR
01765 650183
cycopathcycles.co.uk

Leyburn Bike Repairs
Moor Road, Leyburn, DL8 5DJ
01969 623565

John H Gill & Sons
1 Leeming Lane, Leeming Bar, DL7 9AB
01677 422127
jhgill.gbr.cc